W9-AZI-030

Chronology of Wars

JOHN S. BOWMAN

☑®
Facts On File, Inc.

Note on Photos
Many of the illustrations and photographs used in this book are old,
historical images. The quality of the prints is not always up to modern
standards, as in some cases the originals are from glass negatives or are damaged.
The content of the illustrations, however, made their inclusion important
despite problems in reproduction.

Chronology of Wars
Copyright © 2003 by John S. Bowman
Maps on pages 5, 23, 29, 36, 41, 50, 54, 57, 76, 88, 106, 108, 114, 127, 129, 137, 141,
152, 163, 185, and 205 copyright © 2003 by Facts On File
Map on p. 100 copyright © 2002 Carl Waldman and Facts On File

Facts On File, Inc.
132 West 31st Street
New York NY 10001

Library of Congress Cataloging-in-Publication Data
Bowman, John Stewart, 1931–
Chronology of wars / by John S. Bowman.
v. cm. — (America at war)
Includes bibliographical references and index.
Contents: 1. The Revolutionary War. — 2. The War of 1812. — 3. The United States-
Mexican War. — 4. The Civil War. — 5. Plains Indians Wars. — 6. The Spanish-
American War. — 7. World War I. — 8. World War II. — 9. The Korean War. —
10. The Vietnam War. — 11. The Gulf War.
ISBN 0-8160-4941-6
1. United States—History, Military—To 1900—Chronology—Juvenile literature.
2. United States—History, Military—20th century—Chronology—Juvenile
literature. [1. United States—History, Military. 2. War.] I. Title. II. Series.
E181 .B76 2003
355' .00973—dc21   2002009558

Facts On File books are available at special discounts when purchased in bulk
quantities for businesses, associations, institutions, or sales promotions. Please call
our Special Sales Department in New York at (212) 967-8800 or (800) 322-8755.

You can find Facts On File on the World Wide Web at http://www.factsonfile.com

Text design by Erika K. Arroyo
Logo design by Smart Graphics
Maps by Jeremy Eagle

Printed in the United States of America

MP FOF 10 9 8 7 6 5 4 3 2 1

This book is printed on acid-free paper.

Contents

Acknowledgments

The editor would like to thank Samuel Willard Crompton for providing chronologies of the Revolutionary War, the War of 1812, the U.S.-Mexican War, the Civil War, the Plains Indian Wars, World War I, World War II, the Korean War, and the Persian Gulf War; and Brooks Robards for providing the chronology of the Vietnam War.

Introduction

No nation, no people, likes to think of itself as engaged in fighting wars. Yet wars have been an inseparable part of human history, and the United States can claim no exemption from this reality. The challenge, then, when considering the wars that one's own nation has fought, is to confront three issues. First, how and why did the country go to war—what were its motives for entering it? Second, how did the country conduct itself during the war—did it fight within some basic rules of fairness, even a sense of humaneness? And finally, what were the results of the war—did these in any way justify the losses and suffering?

These are the underlying, if unstated, questions that the America at War set intends to ask its readers. Each of the other 11 volumes deals with one of the major wars fought by the citizens of the United States (although, strictly speaking, the first—the Revolutionary War—was fought by American colonists before they had formed the United States). And each volume is designed both to illuminate and examine its war as a reflection of broader themes in U.S. history.

Approaching the history of any nation via its wars would not be recommended these days if all these books did was to glorify the nation's martial exploits. This notion has been largely rejected along with its close relative, the "Great Man" approach to history. That is, the notion that history has been largely made and is best illuminated by emperors and kings and presidents and strong leaders—almost always males and very often with military credentials.

The America at War set most decidedly does not endorse either of these now generally discredited approaches to history. Rather, these books treat war as a much broader social phenomenon. They place each war in its complete historical contexts—geopolitical and economic, international and diplomatic, domestic and political, technological and scientific, societal and cultural. At the same time, these books in no way slight the events on the fields of combat; they face up to the destruction and bloodshed, the casualties and costs—and to the dedication, sacrifice, and courage that wars have called out from both civilians and the military. The realities of wars are not shirked, but the ideals are not denied.

Each of the other 11 books in the set weaves all these strands into patterned tapestries, but precisely because of the rich texture of such narrative histories, it was determined that it would be beneficial to provide a final volume to separate out some of the basic threads of these wars. That is exactly what this volume does, as a chronology of all 11 wars. *Chronology* derives from two Greek words—*chronos,* meaning "time," and *logos,* meaning "study of." This chronology separates and sets down the events of each war in the exact sequence in which they occurred, usually assigned to the exact day, but occasionally only the month or season when these are sufficient and relevant. Each war's day-by-day chronology is preceded by the briefest of backgrounds that focus on the situations that led directly to the outbreak of war. At the end of each chronology, a section called "Results" provides the casualty figures, material costs, and a brief summary of the results in the broader sense—the war's impact on the peoples and nations involved and on the larger progress of history.

Although the chronologies do provide some details relative to the various dimensions referred to above—diplomatic, international, home front, social, and so on—they cannot attempt to match the narrative accounts of the other 11 volumes in such matters. Put another way, in this chronology the concept of war is more literal, more specifically focused on the hostilities on the land, sea, and air. This volume provides a strong foundation and framework for understanding these wars.

This does raise the question, though, of just what purpose a chronology serves. What does it add to, what advantages does it offer compared with, complete narrative accounts and in-depth analyses?

The first contribution of such a chronology, of course, is simply to serve as a handy reference text, to make accessible as much data as possible in a clear, concise fashion. As such, this chronology becomes a "fact-checking" instrument, useful for those who feel they know something about a war or wars but need a quick check-up, and useful to those who realize they do not know even the most basic facts about a war or wars.

INTRODUCTION

Beyond the straightforward record of facts, a chronology provides a visual, almost tangible sense of the sheer number of days, weeks, months, and years that the United States has been engaged in wars. In fact, the set and the chronology focus on only the 11 major wars. There have been many smaller ones, even excluding the many wars fought by colonists before the Revolutionary War itself—the Barbary Wars, many Indian wars other than the Plains Indian Wars, and in recent times, a whole series of hostilities if not outright wars such as that in former Yugoslavia (Kosovo). One way to look at this is made explicit by this chronology: Between 1775 (when the American Revolution began) and 1991 (when the Persian Gulf War ended) these 11 major wars alone have engaged the United States for about 30 percent of those years. Just turning page after page in a chronology such as this makes this point more graphic.

Another accomplishment of the chronological approach is one that even the best narratives and analyses cannot accomplish: letting the reader experience events exactly as they occurred in time. Wherever, however, wars take place in a continuum of time; bulletins, news reports, headlines are encountered as events take place. Inevitably, when historians later write about these events, they step away from that rigid time frame and tend to extract patterns, topics, themes. Of course this is most valuable, even necessary, but it is also valuable and necessary to realize exactly how events unfolded. To single out one example: Between 1812 and 1814, when the War of 1812 was being fought, citizens and military personnel did not experience a series of separate and isolated "chapters"—a war in the Northwest, a war in the Niagara area, a war on Lake Champlain, a war on the high seas, a war in the Southeast, a war in the Chesapeake Bay area. Americans were experiencing all those "chapters" simultaneously. Only a chronology brings this aspect of wars to the foreground.

Finally and most important, as a teaching/learning tool, a chronology serves to allow students to extract their own patterns and meanings, to come to some insights and conclusions of their own. Here are the facts of that war as they happened over time: What significance can be drawn from this? In particular, a chronology allows readers to consider the three issues posed at the beginning of this preface as crucial to arriving at a judgment about a nation's wars.

The first of these issues—how and why a nation goes into a particular war—narrative histories are admittedly good at explaining. But following the early events in a chronology allows the reader to question just how necessary the outbreak of hostilities was. What were the alternatives? Were they really available at the time—and in "real time"? Are certain individuals to blame? Did everyone with authority do all that might have been done? What was the role of communications, both in the most literal sense of messages, written or spoken, and in the broader sense of willingness to speak and listen to one another?

Several of these wars perhaps seem to have come about through sheer failure of communications—that is, it simply took too much time for messages to reach a potential opponent. Sometimes messages were misunderstood—as when Secretary of State Dean Acheson seemed to be saying that the United States did not regard Korea as within its zone of defense, or when the U.S. ambassador to Iraq seemed to be telling Saddam Hussein that the United States did not regard Kuwait as a territory it would defend. Or what about the many treaties with Native Americans: What messages did each party believe they were sending? How many of these 11 wars seem to be *"just"* wars in the sense that this word is now applied: a war fought for causes that a large part of the world's population would agree made the war necessary. There is no end of questions that might be considered upon a close reading of the chronologies of the early phases of these wars.

Then once a war is underway, a new set of questions arises, and a chronology can help readers arrive at some answers as to how it was fought. Does it appear that this war was fought fairly by one or both sides? Were the rules of war—at least as understood at that time—observed? That is, did they fight with any sense of constraints, of limits? (The occasional use of the term *massacre* suggests that this was not always the case.) Were the appropriate weapons used? Were atrocities committed (and is there any possible justification for such conduct in the heat of battle)?

Beyond laying out those very tangible means of conducting a war, chronologies can raise questions about the broader means. Were strategies and tactics designed to limit casualties—on both sides—or simply to wipe out the most enemy possible? This then raises questions about the leadership in these wars, both by civilians and the military. Does it appear that those making the decisions were well informed and well prepared? Was there good communication among the various leaders? In a word, did each side fight intelligently? Over and over again in these wars, the chronologies reveal instances of U.S. leaders who made faulty

INTRODUCTION

decisions that resulted in tremendous casualties—in the case of Custer, including his own men and himself. Yet Custer was not the only leader to make a bad decision, to fight in an unnecessarily costly manner. Other wars provide examples of ambitious and very costly campaigns that seem, at least in retrospect, to have been wasteful if not downright reckless.

Identifying these occasions can be one of the challenges presented by these chronologies. They also can lead to another and still more fascinating exercise: the great "what ifs" of wars. What if the Confederate forces had quickly marched on Washington, D.C., after their July 1861 victory at the First Battle of Bull Run (Manassas)? Or what if the Union forces had followed up on their several major victories along the way—Antietam in September 1862 or certainly Gettysburg on July 1863? What if General MacArthur, after his triumph at Inchon, Korea, had sent his forces straight across the peninsula and cut off the North Korean forces? Almost all wars provide "what ifs," and chronologies provide an excellent means to reconsider their realities.

And then there is the third great issue—did the end of the war produce results that justify it in any sense? Did either the immediate or eventual results warrant all the lives lost? Perhaps the most persistent example of such a question involves the decision to drop the atomic bombs on Japan to end World War II. Some argue that nothing justified this, but others claim that in fact many more hundreds of thousands of lives—both Allied and Japanese—were saved by the use of such a weapon. Some would go even further and propose that, at the cost of two bombs, the world has learned to avoid the use of nuclear weapons in any future conflict. A chronology cannot settle this question, but it can set forth the situation in real time and support a meaningful discussion.

A concomitant of this examination of results is the examination of how a war ended and questioning if it might have ended much earlier. Did surrender demands made by a side that was "winning" extend the war? This has been said of the Civil War and of the Vietnam War—and for that matter, of World War II. Then, once the terms were agreed on, were they inappropriate and unrealistic? This has been said of the terms imposed on Germany after World War I and also of the terms that the United States allowed Iraq after the Gulf War. Close reading of the chronologies may allow students to raise new questions about such claims.

Perhaps the most compelling question raised by this last issue—do results justify the losses and suffering?—is the one that returns to the opening statement of this preface: No nation or people wants to think of engaging in wars. Going back over these 11 wars, readers might well ask themselves: Had the Revolutionary War never been fought, would Americans still be content to be part of the British Commonwealth like Australia or Canada? Had the war with Mexico never been fought, would Americans today be content to see Mexico still owning all that territory? Had the Civil War not been fought, how many Americans today would accept a separate Confederate nation? Had the Spanish-American War not been fought, would Americans—not to mention Cubans and Puerto Ricans—be satisfied to see those islands as Spanish possessions? Most people feel that the possible results of not having fought World War II are beyond human comprehension. But Korea and Vietnam—suppose the United States had not chosen to enter those wars: What might the world be like today? As for the many wars with American Indians, no chronology, no history book of any kind, can resolve the question of what might have been or whether the results are "justifiable."

What this chronology can provide, though, is a clear compass to steer readers through the events of those and the other wars treated in the America at War set. Although this volume clearly belongs with the 11 other volumes in the set, it can stand as an independent work. Its own glossary defines the technical terms or unusual words that are used throughout the chronologies, for which its maps and illustrations provide graphic supplements. The reading list, meanwhile, is intended to add a whole new dimension to the series by identifying historical atlases and reference works that allow students to pursue these wars in greater depth and by singling out select titles that step back somewhat from the narrative accounts of individual wars and provide perspectives on broader issues. All in all, this chronology volume serves as both the capstone to the America at War set and a portal into the facts and issues that attend these 11 major wars.

1

THE REVOLUTIONARY WAR

In the 13 colonies established along the Atlantic seaboard between 1607 and 1733, the American colonists were accustomed to a large measure of self-government. Even so, most of these colonists supported the British in the series of wars against the French and Indians in North America. The last of these, the French and Indian War (1754–63) ended with the Treaty of Paris, which made Britain the dominant power in North America. In the wake of that new role, however, as Britain began to impose a series of new laws and taxes, many colonists began to question whether remaining under British government and law was the best possible alternative.

1763

- *October 7:* King George III signs the Proclamation of 1763. It limits the line of non-Indian settlement to the headwaters of the rivers that run east to the Atlantic Ocean. No British colonists are supposed to settle beyond that line, which is roughly equivalent to the crest of the Appalachian Mountains.

1764

- *April 5:* King George III signs the Revenue Act, also called the Sugar Act. It allows for vigorous collection of duties on molasses and sugar.

1765

- *March 22:* King George III signs the Stamp Act. Colonists will be required to purchase official stamps that certify such items as major documents and newspapers.
- *May 30:* Patrick Henry proposes seven resolutions (the Virginia Resolves), setting forth complaints against Britain's taxation policies. Virginia's House of Burgesses adopts the first four, but rejects the other three.
- *October 7–25:* Convoked by Massachusetts, nine of the colonies send delegates to a Stamp Act Congress that meets in New York City. The delegates declare that the stamp taxes cannot be collected without the colonists' assent. By this time, British colonial officials are being harassed throughout the colonies.

1766

- *January 14–March 4:* Parliament weighs the state of North American affairs, in particular the hostile response to the Stamp Act.
- *March 18:* King George III assents to Parliament's repeal of the Stamp Act. But the king also assents to the Declaratory Act, which reasserts the right of the king and Parliament to make laws that bind the colonies "in all cases whatsoever."
- *Summer:* Colonists rejoice over the Stamp Act's repeal and choose to ignore the threatening implication of the Declaratory Act.

1767

- *July 2:* King George III signs the Townshend Duties bill. Developed by Prime Minister Charles Townshend, the bill places duties on paper, paint, glass, lead, and tea.

1768

- *October:* British troops arrive in Boston. Under the Quartering Act of 1765, the colonists are not only requited to provide quarters for these troops, they must also pay all costs associated with stationing troops in the colonies.

1770

- *March 5:* Parliament repeals all the Townshend duties except the one on tea.

Crispus Attucks, one of the first American casualties of the American Revolution, is killed during the Boston Massacre, March 5, 1770. *(Library of Congress, Prints & Photographs Division [LC-USZ62-55356])*

- *March 5:* British soldiers, guarding the Customs House in Boston, fire on a mob that has provoked them with taunts, snowballs, and threats. Five American colonists are killed. One of them is Crispus Attucks, the first African American dto die in the revolutionary cause. The event is widely publicized through an engraving by Paul Revere and is soon called the Boston Massacre.
- *December 4:* Two of the seven British soldiers who participated in the Boston Massacre are found guilty of manslaughter. Their thumbs are branded as punishment.

1772

- *June 9:* Rhode Island Patriots burn the British revenue cutter *Gaspée,* which has run aground while pursuing smugglers. No Americans are willing to come forward and testify, so the offenders escape without punishment.
- *November 2:* Boston Patriots create an organization called the Committee of Correspondence, intended to facilitate communication

between the colonists and colonies. By 1774, 10 of the 13 colonies will have such a committee.

1773

- *May:* Parliament passes the East India Company Act. Designed to save the company from bankruptcy, the act makes the tea inexpensive for Americans but keeps a threepenny tax on each pound of tea.
- *November:* Three merchant ships carrying tea arrive in Boston Harbor.
- *December 16:* Two hundred colonists, dressed as Indians, board the three tea ships in Boston Harbor. The colonists dump 342 chests of tea into the harbor, then escape. No one is ever found or charged with the crime. Colonists soon call it the Boston Tea Party.

1774

- *March 31:* King George III gives his assent to the Boston Port Act. Boston Harbor is closed to all shipping until the tea destroyed in December 1773 is paid for. This act is the first of several Parliamentary acts that the British call the Coercive Acts: The Americans call them the Intolerable Acts.
- *May 14:* Gen. Thomas Gage arrives in Boston. He is the new military governor for the Province of Massachusetts Bay.
- *June–December:* Wagonloads of food and clothing arrive in Boston, sent by citizen groups from the other colonies. Without this aid, Boston might soon have been starved into submission by the Port Act.
- *September 5–October 26:* The First Continental Congress meets in Philadelphia. Delegates from 12 of the 13 colonies attend. It denounces the various acts passed by Parliament and calls for ceasing all trade with Britain, but it does not call for revolution.
- *December 13–14:* Boston Patriot leader Paul Revere rides to Portsmouth, New Hampshire, to warn colonists that the British are planning to seize gunpowder, cannons, and small arms at nearby Fort William and Mary. The next day some 400 New Hampshire militiamen successfully assault the fort—defended by six invalided soldiers—in what might be regarded as the first exchange of gunfire of the Revolution.

1775

- *March 23:* At the Second Virginia Convention, held to show support for a Continental Congress, Patrick Henry is alleged to have

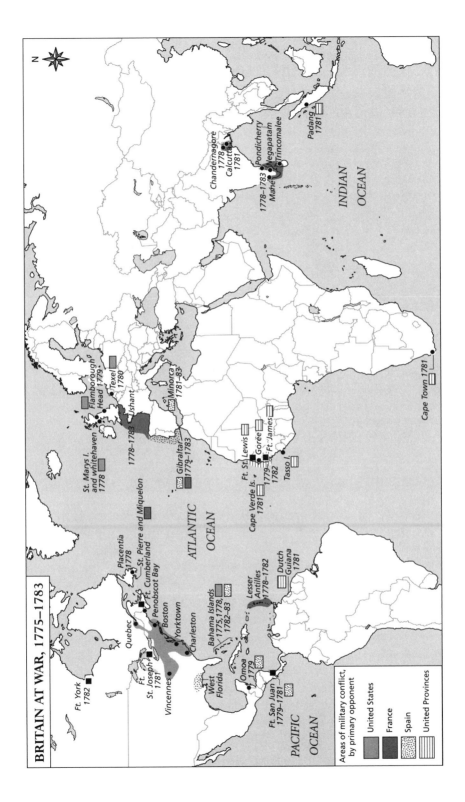

BRITAIN AT WAR, 1775–1783

N

PACIFIC OCEAN

ATLANTIC OCEAN

INDIAN OCEAN

Ft. York 1782
Quebec
Ft. St. Joseph 1781
Placentia 1778
St. Pierre and Miquelon
Ft. Cumberland
Penobscot Bay
Boston
Yorktown
Charleston
Vincennes
Bahama Islands 1775, 1778, 1782–83
West Florida
Omoa 1779
Ft. San Juan 1779–1781
Lesser Antilles 1778–1782
Dutch Guiana 1781

St. Marys I. and Whitehaven 1778
Flamborough Head 1779
Texel 1780
Ushant
1778–1783
Minorca 1781–83
Gibraltar 1779–1783
Cape Verde Is. 1781
Ft. St. Lewis
Gorée 1779
Ft. James 1782
Tasso I.

Chandernagore 1778
Calcutta
Pondicherry
Mahé 1778–1783
Negapatam
Trincomalee 1781
Padang 1781

Cape Town 1781

Areas of military conflict, by primary opponent
United States
France
Spain
United Provinces

Washington takes command of the Continental army at Cambridge, Massachusetts, July 3, 1775. *(National Archives, Still Pictures Branch, NWDNS-148-GW-571)*

declaimed: "I know not what course others may take, but as for me, give me liberty or give me death!"

- *April 14:* General Gage receives orders from London. He is to confiscate the Massachusetts Patriots' powder and ball (ammunition).
- *April 18:* Twelve hundred British soldiers are ferried across the Charles River to Cambridge, Massachusetts. They begin the march to Lexington. Not far ahead of them are three "midnight riders": Paul Revere, Dr. Samuel Prescott, and William Dawes. The efforts of these three men rouse the farmers of Middlesex County during the night. Other riders alert communities north and south of Boston.
- *April 19:* The battles of Lexington and Concord. The British arrive at Lexington Green at 7 A.M. About 70 American militiamen are on the green. Someone fires a shot (no one knows who or on which side) and a skirmish occurs. Seven Americans are killed; the others disperse. The British push on to Concord. Arriving at Concord, the British burn American supplies. In the early afternoon, Americans advance toward Concord Bridge. A skirmish is fought and the British with-

draw. On their long march back to Cambridge, the British lose nearly 300 men killed, wounded, and missing. The Revolution has begun.

- *May:* About 12,000 American militiamen bottle up the British in Boston.
- *May 10:* Ethan Allen and Benedict Arnold surprise the British at Fort Ticonderoga on Lake Champlain in New York and capture the fort and its valuable arms.
- *May 10:* The Second Continental Congress convenes in Philadelphia.
- *May 22:* Three new British generals arrive in Boston: William Howe, Henry Clinton, and John Burgoyne.
- *June 17:* Battle of Bunker Hill: American soldiers seize and fortify Breed's Hill, which overlooks Boston harbor. The British decide on a frontal assault to dislodge the Americans. Gen. William Howe leads the British in three costly frontal attacks. By day's end the British have retaken Breeds Hill, at the cost of 1,054 men killed, wounded, and missing.
- *June 27:* The Continental Congress authorizes an invasion of British Canada (Quebec). It is hoped that the French Canadians, conquered

The troops under Brig. Gen. Richard Montgomery depart Fort Ticonderoga, New York, on their ill-fated campaign to conquer Quebec, August 27, 1775. *(Library of Congress, Prints & Photographs Division [LC-USZ62-108230])*

by Britain in 1760, will join the American cause and become the "Fourteenth Colony."

- *July 3:* George Washington of Virginia arrives in Cambridge to take command of the Continental army.
- *August 27:* Gen. Richard Montgomery sails from Fort Ticonderoga, headed north on Lake Champlain. The campaign for the "Fourteenth Colony"—Canada—has begun.
- *September 13:* Benedict Arnold leaves Newburyport, Massachusetts, with 1,200 men. Arnold and his troops will endure a grueling march through Maine on their way to attack Quebec City.
- *October 13:* The Continental Congress approves the purchase of two 10-gun ships. This is the beginning of the Continental navy.
- *November 9:* Arnold and 600 men emerge on the south bank of the St. Lawrence River, opposite Quebec. They have made one of the great forced marches of the war, indeed of military history.
- *November 10:* The Continental Congress approves the establishment of a marine corps (the Continental Marines) to complement the new Continental Navy.

The USS *Alfred,* first battleship of the U.S. Navy, flies the original flag of the united colonies, the "Grand Union." *(National Archives, Still Pictures Branch, NWDNS-19-N-9977)*

- *November 13:* American general Montgomery enters Montreal, which has surrendered to his men. Quebec now is the only major town in Canada still under British control.
- *December 2–January 1776:* Montgomery and Arnold link forces and commands in front of Quebec City. The city is defended by Gen. Guy Carleton.
- *December 5:* American colonel Henry Knox arrives at Ticonderoga and begins to direct the loading of about 60 pieces of artillery on sleds. On about December 18, the troops set off with the ox-drawn sleds intending to make their way through the winter snow to Boston.
- *December 31:* Benedict Arnold and James Montgomery attack Quebec City. Montgomery is killed in the early fighting. Arnold and many of his men enter the town but are cut off by British troops who use barricades. Arnold is wounded but escapes. Col. Daniel Morgan is taken prisoner.

1776

- *January 10:* British political writer Thomas Paine, who came to America one year earlier, publishes his *Common Sense,* a pamphlet advocating independence from Britain. It soon sells more than 100,000 copies.
- *January 24:* Henry Knox and his men arrive at Cambridge with what Knox calls a "noble train of artillery."
- *February 27:* Patriots and Loyalists clash at Moore's Creek near Wilmington, North Carolina. The Patriots win a resounding victory.
- *March 4–5:* American soldiers take and fortify Dorchester Heights, just south of the city of Boston. The Americans position the cannons brought by Henry Knox from Ticonderoga.
- *March 10:* British general Howe agrees to leave Boston.
- *March 17:* The last of the British and their Loyalist supporters sail from Boston, which is now a free American city.
- *April 6:* In the first naval engagement involving the Continental navy and a British ship, Commodore Esek Hopkins on his flagship, the *Alfred,* leads a squadron of eight ships against the HMS *Glasgow* off the coast of Connecticut. The *Alfred* suffers more casualties and damage than the *Glasgow,* and Hopkins will be court-martialed for letting the British get away. In charge of the main gun deck on the *Alfred* was young lieutenant John Paul Jones.

- *May 9–16:* A small squadron of American ships takes and briefly occupies Nassau in the Bahamas.
- *May:* Benedict Arnold's forces retreat from Quebec and Canada.
- *June 7:* Virginia delegate Richard Henry Lee proposes to the Continental Congress that the colonies should now become and declare themselves to be "free and independent States."
- *June 28:* A British squadron bombards Fort Moultrie in the harbor of Charles Town, South Carolina. The fort's garrison withstands the bombardment and inflicts serious damage to some of the British ships. South Carolina will later be known as the Palmetto State, partly in honor of the fort's palmetto logs.
- *July 2:* Gen. William Howe disembarks at Staten Island, New York. Howe has more than 30,000 British and Hessian (German) soldiers. The naval arm is commanded by his brother, Adm. Richard Howe.
- *July 4:* The Second Continental Congress officially endorses the Declaration of Independence. Although designed by a four-man committee, the declaration's text is mostly the words of Thomas Jefferson of Virginia.
- *August 27:* General Howe wins the Battle of Long Island. Washington's troops are penned in on the island's western extremity.
- *August 28–29:* Washington's American soldiers are ferried across the East River to Manhattan. The naval operation is performed by the regiment of Marblehead Volunteers, commanded by David Glover.
- *September 9:* American inventor David Bushnell pilots his primitive submarine, *Turtle,* around British ships in New York Harbor. Bushnell fails to gain the right position; he had hoped to drill holes in enemy ships.
- *September 11:* American commissioners, led by Benjamin Franklin, meet Admiral Howe on Staten Island. When they learn that Howe has been empowered only to offer pardons, the Americans break off the negotiation.
- *September 15:* The British attack Manhattan Island. Washington and his men retreat to Harlem Heights on the northern part of the island.
- *September 22:* Capt. Nathan Hale is hanged by the British in New York. Hale, a captain in the Continental army, had been caught out of uniform and is executed as a spy. His last words are alleged to be: "I only regret that I have but one life to lose for my country."

THE REVOLUTIONARY WAR

- *October 11:* In the Battle of Valcour Bay, Benedict Arnold fights and loses a naval battle on Lake Champlain. Although he loses the day, Arnold keeps his fleet in position throughout the summer and thereby prevents a possible invasion from Canada that year.
- *November 16:* Hessian soldiers storm and capture Fort Washington on the northern tip of Manhattan Island.
- *November 20:* American troops abandon Fort Lee on the west bank of the Hudson just minutes before the arrival of British and Hessian soldiers.
- *December 7:* Washington leads 4,000 men, all that remain of his earlier 20,000, across the Delaware River. The British leave 4,000 Hessian troops (German mercenaries) on the east bank of the Delaware to keep an eye on Washington during the winter.
- *December 21:* Benjamin Franklin arrives in Paris and initiates his connection to the Court of King Louis XVI.
- *December 23:* Thomas Paine publishes *The Crisis,* which begins with the line: "These are the times that try men's souls."

Benjamin Franklin served as a diplomat, representing the colonies at the court of France. *(National Archives, Still Pictures Branch, NWDNS-66-G-15B-5)*

Gen. George Washington inspects preparations beside the Delaware River on December 25, 1776, hours before the Continental army's surprise night attack on the Hessians at the Battle of Trenton. *(Library of Congress, Prints & Photographs Division [LC-USZ62-61047])*

- *December 25:* The Hessians at Trenton, New Jersey, celebrate Christmas. Washington has planned a "Christmas gamble" under which he will attack the unsuspecting foe the next day.
- *December 26:* The Battle of Trenton: Washington crosses the Delaware River at night and surprises the Hessians in Trenton at dawn. Washington takes 1,000 prisoners and suffers few losses of his own.

1777

- *January 2:* Washington has gone on the attack and at Princeton, New Jersey, defeats the British under General Cornwallis.
- *January 6:* Washington leads his men into winter quarters at Morristown, New Jersey.
- *May 11:* British general John Burgoyne arrives in Montreal, Quebec. Burgoyne has proposed—and London has accepted—a plan for three British armies to converge on Albany, New York, this summer and hold the line of the Hudson River. If they succeed, the British will split

New England off from the other rebellious colonies. Burgoyne is to march straight south from Canada; Howe is to march north from New York City; and Col. Barry St. Leger is to cross Lake Ontario and arrive at Albany by way of the Mohawk River.

- *June 20:* The marquis de Lafayette arrives in Philadelphia and offers his service to the Continental Congress.
- *July 5–7:* Burgoyne captures Fort Ticonderoga on Lake Champlain.
- *July 23:* General Howe and 20,000 British troops leave New York City aboard the British fleet and transports and head south for Chesapeake Bay. Whether Howe never received orders from London to rendezvous at Albany, or if he simply chose to disregard such orders, has never been fully established. But his departure deprives Burgoyne's plan of the largest of the three British forces.
- *August 3:* British Colonel St. Leger places Fort Stanwix in Upstate New York under siege.
- *August 6:* British and Loyalist forces ambush a Patriot force intended to relieve the garrison at Fort Stanwix. The Battle of Oriskany is noted for the fierce conduct on both sides.

Washington used the Ford mansion in Morristown, New Jersey, as his headquarters during the winter of 1776–77. *(Library of Congress, Prints & Photographs Division [LC-D4-90029])*

CHRONOLOGY OF WARS

Continental militiamen destroy a foraging party of 900 men from General Burgoyne's army in the Battle of Bennington, Vermont, August 16, 1777. *(National Archives, Still Pictures Branch, NWDNS-111-SC-96740)*

- *August 16:* The Battle of Bennington, Vermont: New Hampshire and Vermont militiamen defeat two columns of Hessians sent by General Burgoyne to obtain supplies.
- *August 22:* Colonel St. Leger ends the siege of Fort Stanwix and heads back to British Canada. His Indian allies had begun to desert him, leaving him without the scouts he needed for his campaign.
- *September 11:* General Howe has marched his troops north from Chesapeake Bay and they defeat the Americans at the Battle of Brandywine River, Pennsylvania. The marquis de Lafayette is wounded in the battle.
- *September 19:* The First Battle of Saratoga, New York: Burgoyne's army is stopped by a formidable combination of American Continentals and militiamen. Col. Daniel Morgan's riflemen play a significant role.
- *September 26:* British troops enter Philadelphia, Pennsylvania, former seat of the Continental Congress.
- *October 4:* The Battle of Germantown, Pennsylvania: Washington makes a surprise attack on the British. The Americans experience

early success, but they are thwarted by the British defense of the Chew House, a stone house, and by a morning fog that throws their columns into confusion.

- *October 7:* The Second Battle of Saratoga: Burgoyne makes an attack but is quickly thrown on the defensive. Benedict Arnold leads a charge that captures the main British redoubt, but Arnold is wounded in the leg, the same leg that was wounded at Quebec in 1775.
- *October 17:* Burgoyne and his men, 6,000 in all, lay down their arms at Saratoga. Under the terms of the Convention of Saratoga, Burgoyne will be repatriated to England.
- *December 19:* Washington leads his men into winter quarters at Valley Forge, Pennsylvania. Here they will endure weeks of the hardships of winter while the British enjoy a festive season in Philadelphia.

1778

- *February 6:* France signs a treaty of alliance with the United States. The architects of the treaty are French foreign minister Vergennes and Benjamin Franklin, American emissary to the court at Versailles.
- *April 10–May 8:* John Paul Jones, a Scottish sailor who has cast his lot with the American revolutionaries, takes his *Ranger* on around the eastern coast of England and Scotland, at one point (April 23) actually landing at the English town of Whitehaven. On April 24 he defeats the British *Drake* and takes it to a port in France.
- *May 30:* Iroquois Indians, allied with the British, attack Cobleskill, New York. The Iroquois are split between the Mohawk and Seneca, who favor the British, the Oneida, who favor the Americans, and the Onondaga, who remain neutral. Most of the Cayugas favor the British, while most of the Tuscaroras favor the Americans.
- *June 18:* British general Henry Clinton, who has replaced General Howe, evacuates Philadelphia. The British head across New Jersey on their way to New York City.
- *June 19:* Washington leads his men out of their quarters at Valley Forge. The Americans pursue the British across New Jersey.
- *June 28:* At the Battle of Monmouth Courthouse in New Jersey, Washington nearly defeats the British in a pitched battle. The American plan is foiled by Gen. Charles Lee, who shows timidity. Washington arrives in time to rally the Americans, but the best he can manage is a draw. During the fighting, an American cannoneer is wounded;

his wife, who has been carrying water to the troops, is said to have taken his place. It is claimed that she is Mary Ludwig Hays McCauley, and she is said to have been the first to have been called "Molly Pitcher."

- *June 30:* George Rogers Clark sets off down the Ohio River with some 200 volunteers, the beginning of his epic trip into Illinois to attack the British and their Indian allies there.
- *July 4:* George Rogers Clark captures the British fort at Kaskaskia in the Illinois country.
- *July 10:* A large French war fleet, led by the count d'Estaing, appears near New York Harbor. D'Estaing has the edge in ships and guns, but his captains refuse to cross the shallow sand bar at the harbor's entrance. Chagrined, d'Estaing sails off to besiege Newport, Rhode Island.
- *July 20:* During the so-called Night of the Long Knives ("Long Knives" was the Indians' name for whites who carried hunting knives or bayonets) George Rogers Clark's force occupies the British fort at Vincennes on the Wabash River.
- *August 8–11:* Admiral d'Estaing and American general John Sullivan besiege Newport, Rhode Island. D'Estaing puts out to sea to meet a challenge from the British fleet of Admiral Howe. A storm dismasts many of the ships of both fleets. D'Estaing sails to Boston to refit his ships, and Sullivan is forced to lift his siege of Newport.
- *November 11:* Mohawk chief Joseph Brant and Loyalist Walter Butler lead a devastating raid on American settlements in Cherry Valley, New York.
- *December 17:* British colonel Henry Hamilton (known as "the Hair Buyer" because he allegedly pays Indians for colonists' scalps) reoccupies Fort Vincennes.

1779

- *February 5:* George Rogers Clark leaves Fort Kaskaskia with 170 men. Despite the flood season, Clark intends to retake Fort Vincennes.
- *February 9:* Philadelphia authorities accuse Benedict Arnold (military governor of the city) of corruption and abuse of power. The charges are taken up by Congress, and in 1780 George Washington delivers an official reprimand to Arnold for his conduct.

- *February 25:* Clark recaptures Fort Vincennes. Colonel Hamilton becomes a prisoner of war.
- *June 21:* Spain declares war on Britain. Spain does not conclude an alliance with the United States because it fears that the idea of rebellion might spread to its own colonies.
- *July 15–16:* Gen. Anthony Wayne and his men capture Stony Point, New York, in a silent attack with bayonets.
- *August 12:* The Massachusetts state navy, some 40 ships, is caught in the mouth of Penobscot Bay, Maine. The British squadron proceeds to sink or destroy every Massachusetts ship. Paul Revere, who is second in command of the Americans, will later face a court-martial for his role in failing to stop the sailors from abandoning their ships.
- *August 29:* American general John Sullivan defeats the Iroquois Indians and their Loyalist allies at the Battle of Elmira in Upstate New York. Sullivan proceeds to devastate the crops and towns of the Iroquois Indians who have been supporting the British.
- *September 16:* French admiral D'Estaing calls on the British at Savannah, Georgia, to surrender. When they do not yield, D'Estaing begins a formal siege.
- *September 23:* Capt. John Paul Jones leads the *Bonhomme Richard* to victory over HMS *Serapis.* The British do well in the early fighting, and they call on Jones to yield. He answers: "Surrender? Why sir, I have not yet begun to fight!" The Americans transfer to the captured vessel, and the *Bonhomme Richard* sinks that day.
- *October 9:* The French and Americans make a frontal assault on the British defenses at Savannah. The results are catastrophic: 650 Americans and French are killed, including Count Casimir Pulaski, a Polish volunteer to the American cause.
- *October 17:* Washington leads his troops into winter quarters at Morristown, New Jersey, where they must endure an extremely cold winter.
- *December 26:* Gen. Henry Clinton and 8,700 British troops leave New York, headed for the southern colonies.

1780

- *February 1:* The British fleet and army, led by Clinton, arrive off Charles Town, South Carolina.
- *March 14:* Bernardo Galvez, the Spanish governor of Louisiana, captures the British fort at Mobile, Alabama. Although he is fighting

While cruising the British Isles to disrupt shipping, the American privateer *Bonhomme Richard* captures the British warship *Serapis* on September 23, 1779. *(National Archives, Still Pictures Branch, NWDNS-127-N-A408767)*

the British, Galvez does not coordinate his movements with the Americans.

- *April 8:* British ships sail past Fort Moultrie in the harbor of Charles Town. This movement allows the British to isolate the town from the mainland.
- *May 19:* General Clinton accepts the surrender of Charles Town, South Carolina. Commanded by Gen. Benjamin Lincoln, more than 5,000 men lay down their arms, the largest American surrender during the war.
- *May 29:* British colonel Banastre Tarleton has his dragoons kill more than 100 Americans at the Battle of Waxhaws in South Carolina. Many of the Americans had attempted to surrender. Tarleton's disregard of conventional rules of warfare lead him to be called "Bloody" Tarleton.
- *June 25:* Gen. Horatio Gates, the hero of Saratoga, takes command of what is left of the American army in the southern states.

- *July 11:* French general Rochambeau and 5,000 troops land at Newport, Rhode Island.
- *August 16:* General Cornwallis completely defeats General Gates at the Battle of Camden, South Carolina. Baron de Kalb, a German volunteer, dies fighting heroically, while Gates escapes on horseback. The American cause in the South lies in ruins.
- *August:* Benedict Arnold receives command of West Point. Although he was found at fault in the matter of his governorship of Philadelphia, Arnold remains one of the most visible signs of American heroism.
- *September 23–25:* British major John Andre is captured out of uniform. (Convicted as a spy, he will be hanged on October 2.) His captors find plans for West Point in the soles of his shoes. The trail leads to Gen. Benedict Arnold, commandant of West Point. Arnold escapes to the safety of a British ship and is taken to New York City. His plan to betray the fort for £20,000 has been foiled.
- *October 7:* Battle of King's Mountain, South Carolina. Backcountry Patriots surround and annihilate the Loyalists commanded by British major Patrick Ferguson. The destruction of Ferguson's command persuades General Cornwallis to halt his invasion of North Carolina.
- *December:* Soon after he takes command, Greene divides his small army into two groups: one led by Gen. Daniel Morgan and the other by Greene himself. Although this is contrary to accepted military strategy, Greene believes he may trick the British into making a similar division of their forces.
- *December 2:* Gen. Nathanael Greene arrives at Charlotte, North Carolina, and takes command of all American forces in the South.

1781

- *January:* British general Cornwallis pursues Nathanael Greene while British colonel Tarleton pursues General Morgan's column.
- *January 1–8:* A serious crisis develops in the winter quarters at Morristown, New Jersey, when troops from Pennsylvania effectively mutiny over their poor conditions and lack of pay. Only the adroit actions of Gen. Anthony Wayne put down the mutiny.
- *January 5:* Benedict Arnold, now a British general, takes Richmond, Virginia.
- *January 17:* Battle of Cowpens, South Carolina. General Morgan turns the tables on Colonel Tarleton at the battle, fought on the banks

of the Broad River. In just two hours, Tarleton is completely defeated, and he takes flight.

- *January 20–27:* Units of the New Jersey Continentals mutiny in Pompton, New Jersey. Washington sends 600 men to suppress the mutiny, and two of its leaders are executed.

- *January 24:* General Cornwallis has his men burn their baggage, allowing the troops to move faster, in an effort to catch Nathanael Greene.

- *January 25–February 14:* Greene wins the "Race to the Dan River," a river in North Carolina that provides a major obstacle. The Americans are ferried across just hours before the British arrive. Lacking boats, Cornwallis cannot cross the river.

- *March 1–2:* The Articles of Confederation are ratified, and Congress declares that the Articles are the law of the land. Congress gives itself a new title: The United States in Congress Assembled.

- *March 6:* Washington and French general Rochambeau meet for the first time, in Newport, Rhode Island. Rochambeau defers to Washington as the overall Allied leader.

Col. William Washington leads a cavalry charge, reinforcing the skillful tactics of Gen. Daniel Morgan at the Battle of Cowpens, January 1781.
(National Archives, Still Pictures Branch, NWDNS-148-GW-390)

- *March 15:* Battle of Guilford Courthouse, North Carolina. Greene and Cornwallis clash in a battle known for its savagery. The British win, at the cost of 600 casualties. Charles James Fox, leader of the opposition in the British Parliament, is said to have remarked, "One more such victory would prove the ruin of the British army."
- *April–May:* Discouraged by his inability to defeat Greene, General Cornwallis moves the bulk of his army to Virginia.
- *June 4:* Col. Banastre Tarleton misses by minutes capturing Thomas Jefferson, governor of Virginia.
- *June:* A force of about 5,000 Americans, led by Anthony Wayne and Lafayette, maneuver and feint with Cornwallis's 7,000-man army in Virginia.
- *July 6:* Cornwallis mauls a detachment of Americans at the Battle of Green Spring Farm, Virginia.
- *August 1:* General Cornwallis settles in at Yorktown, Virginia, on the York River and edge of the Chesapeake Bay. Here, Cornwallis believes, he can receive supplies and reinforcements by sea.
- *August 14:* Washington learns that a large French war fleet has left the West Indies, headed for Chesapeake Bay. Although his dearest wish is to recapture New York City, Washington decides to march to Virginia and trap Cornwallis there.
- *August 31:* The French fleet commanded by Admiral de Grasse arrives in Chesapeake Bay.
- *September 5–7:* The naval Battle of the Capes. Admiral de Grasse and the French fleet rebuff an attack by Adm. Thomas Graves's British fleet. De Grasse maintains the crucial control of the entrance to Chesapeake Bay.
- *September 28:* The Franco-American siege of Yorktown begins.
- *October 14:* American and French troops attack and capture two key British redoubts at Yorktown.
- *October 16:* A British sortie against an American redoubt is partially successful. Skillful artillerists soon have the spiked guns firing again, however.
- *October 19:* Cornwallis surrenders. Seven thousand British lay down their arms.
- *November 25:* News of the surrender reaches London. Prime Minister Lord North is said to have responded, "Oh God, it's all over!"
- *December 31:* Congress officially charters the Bank of North America. This is the first central bank in the colonies, which are now states.

U.S. and French commanders convene in Virginia and carry out the siege of Yorktown, September 28–October 19, 1781. *From center to right:* the comte de Rochambeau, George Washington, and the marquis de Lafayette. *(National Archives, Still Pictures Branch, NWDNS-148-GW-516)*

1782

- *March 20:* British prime minister Lord North resigns and is replaced by the marquis of Rockingham.
- *April 6:* British admiral Rodney wins a major naval engagement over French admiral de Grasse at the Battle of the Saintes in the Caribbean. The victory will allow Britain to go to the peace table with its honor intact.
- *April 12:* British delegates arrive in Paris to begin peace negotiations with the American delegates—Benjamin Franklin, John Adams, John Jay, and Henry Laurens.
- *August 19:* The Battle of Blue Licks: American frontier fighters from Kentucky are defeated by Loyalists and Indians at a battle near present-day Lexington, Kentucky.
- *November 10:* Frontier fighters led by George Rogers Clark burn the Shawnee settlement at Chillicothe in present-day Ohio.

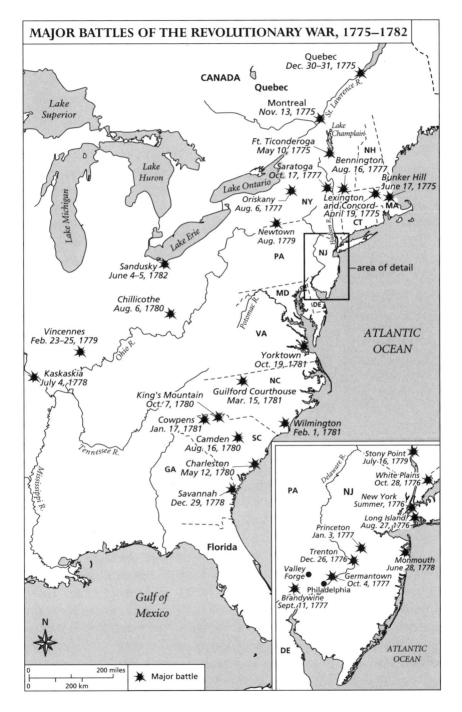

MAJOR BATTLES OF THE REVOLUTIONARY WAR, 1775–1782

Quebec
Dec. 30–31, 1775

CANADA

Quebec

Montreal
Nov. 13, 1775

Lake Superior

St. Lawrence R.

Lake Champlain

Ft. Ticonderoga
May 10, 1775

NH

Bennington
Aug. 16, 1777

Lake Huron

Saratoga
Oct. 17, 1777

Bunker Hill
June 17, 1775

Lake Ontario

Oriskany
Aug. 6, 1777

NY

Lexington
and Concord
April 19, 1775

MA

Lake Michigan

CT

Lake Erie

Newtown
Aug. 1779

PA

NJ

area of detail

Sandusky
June 4–5, 1782

Hudson R.

Chillicothe
Aug. 6, 1780

MD

DE

Vincennes
Feb. 23–25, 1779

Ohio R.

Potomac R.

VA

ATLANTIC
OCEAN

Yorktown
Oct. 19, 1781

Kaskaskia
July 4, 1778

NC

King's Mountain
Oct. 7, 1780

Guilford Courthouse
Mar. 15, 1781

Cowpens
Jan. 17, 1781

Wilmington
Feb. 1, 1781

Tennessee R.

Camden
Aug. 16, 1780

SC

Stony Point
July 16, 1779

Charleston
May 12, 1780

GA

Delaware R.

White Plains
Oct. 28, 1776

Mississippi R.

Savannah
Dec. 29, 1778

PA

NJ

New York
Summer, 1776

Long Island
Aug. 27, 1776

Princeton
Jan. 3, 1777

Florida

Trenton
Dec. 26, 1776

Monmouth
June 28, 1778

Valley
Forge

Germantown
Oct. 4, 1777

Gulf of
Mexico

Philadelphia

Brandywine
Sept. 11, 1777

N

DE

ATLANTIC
OCEAN

| 0 | 200 miles |
| 0 | 200 km |

✶ Major battle

- *November 30:* American and British peace commissioners sign preliminary articles of peace. French leaders are astounded at the generous terms Britain offers the Americans: The boundary between the United States and Canada is drawn at the 45th parallel of latitude, and the British yield their claim to land south of the Great Lakes. French minister Vergennes later comments: "The British buy the peace."
- *December 5:* King George III makes a speech in which he declares he is ready to regard the former colonies as "free and independent states."

1783

- *January 20:* Preliminary articles of peace are signed by Britain, France, and Spain. Britain gives up all claims to the land from the Atlantic to the Mississippi and from Canada to Georgia. France gains very little for its involvement except some fishing rights off Newfoundland; Spain wins back Florida and Minorca, but not Gibraltar as it hoped.
- *April 11:* The Continental Congress expresses satisfaction with the preliminary articles of peace.
- *September 3:* The final articles of peace between Britain and the United States are signed in Paris.
- *November 25:* British general Guy Carleton (who defended Quebec in 1775) and the last British troops evacuate New York City.
- *December 4:* George Washington bids farewell to his officers in an emotional evening at Fraunces Tavern in New York City.

Results

Exact casualty figures for the war are hard to come by. It is generally agreed that some 6,000 colonists died in battle, while at least another 16,000 died of wounds and in British prisons. The British casualties in North America are conservatively estimated at some 4,500. German mercenaries (Hessians) lost another 7,600, while French casualties (mostly sailors) may have been as high as 1,200; American Indians also suffered high casualties. The cost is equally hard to estimate, but it would be in the billions of 21st-century dollars for both nations, and the debt put great pressure on their budgets. The greatest loss, of course, was Britain's—the loss of the 13 colonies and the territory they would claim to their west.

2

THE WAR OF 1812

Great Britain went to war with Napoleonic France in 1803. In the seven years that followed, Britain impressed about 5,000 American seamen, forcing them to serve in the Royal Navy. British officers boarded American ships, questioned seamen, and took off those whom they claim were born in England. The expression used is: "Once an Englishman, always an Englishman." While some of the impressed men were of English birth, many others were Americans who were unfairly taken.

1807

- *June 22:* In the most provocative impressment incident, the British frigate *Leopard* fires on the American frigate *Chesapeake* after its captain refuses to submit to a search. After three of the crew are killed and 18 wounded, the Americans let the British aboard and they take away four men. Many Americans call for war with Britain.
- *December 21:* President Thomas Jefferson's response to the outrage over impressment is to get Congress to pass the Embargo Act, which virtually ends American commerce with other nations. This has a negative impact on U.S. economic life, particular that of the North, and Jefferson's attempts to modify the original act with subsequent embargo acts only aggravates conditions.

1809

- *March 15:* Jefferson concedes that the embargo acts have failed and signs the Non-Intercourse Act, reopening commerce to all nations except Britain and France. During the next two years, this bill's provisions will be alternately enforced and rescinded, but the impact on U.S. commerce continues to be negative.

1811

- Two American Indian brothers, the Shawnee chief Tecumseh and Tenskwatawa (also known as the Shawnee Prophet) have been developing a tribal confederacy, hoping to stop the continued expansion of settlement by white Americans west of the Appalachians. In the summer of 1811, Tecumseh leaves their village, Prophetstown (in present-day Indiana), and travels among the southern tribes, trying to convince them to join the confederacy. Tecumseh has limited success, but a group of younger, ambitious Creek warriors (known as the Red Sticks) are swayed by his oratory. While Tecumseh is on his return journey, Prophetstown is menaced by an army of American militia led by Gen. William Henry Harrison. Tenskwatawa unwisely decides to fight.
- *November 4:* A new U.S. Congress, the 12th, convenes. Angry over alleged British support of the Indians west of the Appalachians, numerous members favor a war with Britain that would allow the United States to seize Canada. They are called the War Hawks.
- *November 7:* The Battle of Tippecanoe (named after the nearby creek) is a standoff, but the Indians abandon Prophetstown, which is burned by Harrison's army. Tecumseh will return to find the town and his confederacy in ruins. Hoping to obtain help and munitions, he crosses the border into British Canada.

1812

- *June 1:* U.S. president James Madison, citing continuing British impressment and their support of Indians such as Tecumseh, calls for a declaration of war on Great Britain.
- *June 4:* The House of Representatives approves the declaration by a vote of 79-49.
- *June 17:* The Senate approves the declaration by a vote of 19-13.
- *June 18:* President Madison signs the declaration of war.
- *June 25:* Definite news arrives in Washington, D.C., that a new British cabinet has rescinded the infamous Orders-in-Council that had formed the basis for impressment. The news does not change events in Washington: War has been declared and will commence.

- *August 15:* The Americans at Fort Dearborn (present-day Chicago), believing the Indians in the area are friendly, evacuate the fort; instead, some 500 warriors attack the group, kill 53 of them, and take some civilians as prisoners.
- *August 16:* American general William Hull surrenders the garrison of Fort Detroit, 2,400 men, to British general Isaac Brock and Chief Tecumseh, who have become allies. It is the largest single American surrender since 1780 when 5,000 men surrendered at Charles Town, South Carolina, to the British.
- *August 19:* The USS *Constitution* wins a resounding victory over HMS *Guerrière* off the coast of Nova Scotia. After the battle, the *Guerrière* is blown up. During the battle, American sailors notice some British cannonballs bouncing off the *Constitution*'s sides and exclaim, "She's got sides of iron!" Later it becomes known as "Old Ironsides." The American commander, Isaac Hull, is a nephew of Gen. William Hull who surrendered at Detroit.
- *September 4–16:* Tecumseh leads a siege of Fort Harrison in what is now Indiana. The garrison, commanded by Capt. Zachary Taylor, holds out until General Harrison arrives, and the siege is lifted.
- *October 13:* Some 600 U.S. troops cross the Niagara River and take Queenstown Heights, in Canada; many American militiamen, however, refuse to cross because they have volunteered only to fight in their own communities. In the ensuing battle with the British forces led by Gen. Isaac Brock, the Americans suffer heavier casualties, but General Brock is killed.
- *October 25:* Under the command of Stephen Decatur, the USS *United States* defeats and captures HMS *Macedonian* off the Madeira Islands. The *Macedonian* is brought to Newport, Rhode Island, the first British man-of-war ever to enter a U.S. port as a prize.
- *November 19:* U.S. general Henry Dearborn reaches the Canadian border on Lake Champlain. Two-thirds of his men inform him they will not cross the border because they are New York State militiamen and have not contracted to fight outside the state. In frustration, Dearborn returns south to Albany.
- *November 20:* Attempting to cover the failure of Gen. Dearborn's operation, Lt. Zebulon Pike leads an attack across the Canadian border, but American troops and militia mistakenly fire on each other and Pike has to withdraw.

The USS *Constitution* defeats the HMS *Guerrière*, August 19, 1812.
(National Archives, Still Pictures Branch, NWDNS-127-N-302108)

- *December 29:* The USS *Constitution* defeats HMS *Java* off the coast of Brazil. The *Java* surrenders after a four-hour battle; it is later burned and sunk.

1813

- *January 22:* American general James Winchester is surprised and defeated by British general Henry Procter in the Battle of Raisin River in what is now Michigan. In the battle and the ensuing attack on those who surrendered, some 400 Americans are casualties. "Remember the Raisin!" becomes a rallying cry for the U.S. Army.
- *March 27:* American captain Oliver Hazard Perry reaches Presque Isle (Pennsylvania) and begins to build a U.S. squadron on the southern shore of Lake Erie.
- *April 27:* U.S. general Zebulon Pike lands troops at York (present-day Toronto) on Lake Ontario. Soon after the Americans take the town, a British powder magazine explodes, killing Pike and some 50 other Americans. Convinced that the explosion had been planned by the enemy, the enraged U.S. troops sack and burn York for the next three days.

THE WAR OF 1812

WAR OF 1812: NAVAL BATTLES, 1812–1815

NORTH ATLANTIC OCEAN

ENGLAND

Wasp/Reindeer 1814

Wasp/Avon 1814

Constitution/ Guerrière 1812

FRANCE

Enterprise/Boxer 1813

Chesapeake/Shannon 1813

SPAIN

President captured

Constitution/Guerrière 1812

UNITED STATES

President Belvidera 1812

Wasp/Frolic 1812

Gibraltar

Constitution/ Cyane

Pursuit of the Constitution

1812 1815

United States/ Macedonian

Gulf of Mexico

U.S.S. Frolic captured

WEST INDIES

Africa

1814

Peacock/Epervier

Caribbean Sea

Hornet/Peacock 1813

SOUTH ATLANTIC OCEAN

PERU

PACIFIC OCEAN

BRAZIL

Constitution/ Java 1812

CHILE

Essex/Phoebe 1814

ARGENTINA

Hornet/Penguin 1815

N

Africa

INDIA

PACIFIC OCEAN

| 0 | 800 miles |
| 0 | 800 km |

Sumatra Java

1815

Peacock/Nautilus

INDIAN OCEAN

Constitution	American ship
Guerrière	British ship
1814	Battle date
✳	Major battle

Hornet/Cornwallis 1815

- **June 1:** The HMS *Shannon* meets and defeats the USS *Chesapeake* outside Boston Harbor. American captain James Lawrence is killed. Among his last words are "Don't give up the ship," which becomes a rallying cry for the U.S. Navy. On that same day, known as the "Infamous First of June," U.S. captain Stephen Decatur is turned back as he attempts to run the British blockade of Long Island Sound. The British navy is starting to gain the upper hand on the Americans.

- *June 5:* Some 2,000 American troops encamped at Stoney Creek, near Hamilton, Ontario, are surprised by British troops early in the morning; although they suffer fewer casualties than the British, two American generals are captured.
- *June 24:* British troops win the Battle of Beaver Dams on the Canadian side of the Niagara River. Four hundred eighty-four Americans surrender to a smaller group of British troops. British morale is restored, and the British Canadians find a new heroine: Laura Secord, who walked some 20 miles through American lines to warn the British commander.
- *July 27:* The Battle of Burnt Corn Creek, north of Pensacola, Florida, is fought between members of the Red Stick faction of the Creek Nation and U.S. militiamen. The Creek win this battle, which inaugurates the Creek War phase of the War of 1812.
- *July 30:* Canadian militia and British troops capture Plattsburgh, New York, and destroy most of its buildings before departing on August 1.

In the Battle of Lake Erie, fought September 10, 1813, Capt. Oliver Perry transformed what seemed like certain defeat into a stunning U.S. victory. *(National Archives, Still Pictures Branch, NWDNS-111-SC-92653)*

The Shawnee leader Tecumseh is killed at the Battle of the Thames, October 5, 1813. Though Tecumseh's body is never found, many subsequently claim responsibility for his death—in this representation, the Kentucky mounted volunteers led by Col. Richard M. Johnson. *(Library of Congress, Prints & Photographs Division [LC-USZ62-10173])*

- *August 30:* Creek warriors surprise and take U.S. Fort Mims in what is now Alabama. Some 400 of the 500 Americans are killed, and this arouses U.S. militiamen to seek out the Creek.
- *September 10:* U.S. commandant Oliver Hazard Perry wins the Battle of Lake Erie when his nine ships defeat a British squadron of the same size. Following the victory, Perry sends a message to Gen. William Henry Harrison: "We have met the enemy and they are ours." This victory makes the British hold of Fort Detroit tenuous.
- *September 27:* General Harrison occupies Fort Detroit. The British and Indians under Gen. Henry Procter and Tecumseh have retreated eastward toward Lake Ontario.
- *October 5:* General Harrison wins the Battle of the Thames River (also known as the Battle of Moraviantown) over the British and Indians. Chief Tecumseh, who had persuaded or shamed General Procter into making a stand, is killed in the battle. His body is never found, and many people will claim that they had killed the great chief. One of them, Richard M. Johnson, will become vice president in 1837.

- *November 9:* Gen. Andrew Jackson leads a force of Tennessee militia to defeat a large group of Creek warriors at the Battle of Talladega in present-day Alabama.
- *November 11:* British troops and Canadian militiamen stop a U.S. force under Gen. Jacob Brown at Chrysler's farm, in Ontario. The British victory restores a measure of British morale and ensures that Montreal is safe for the winter.
- *November 29:* American general John Floyd captures the Creek village of Auttose in present-day Alabama. About 200 Creek are killed and some 400 homes are destroyed.

1814

- *March 27:* Gen. Andrew Jackson wins the Battle of Horseshoe Bend in present-day Alabama. Helped by Cherokee Indian scouts, Jackson surrounds and destroys the Creek fort. The Indians suffer the loss of some 900, most of them warriors, and Chief Red Eagle surrenders himself to Jackson. The Creek War is effectively over.
- *April 6:* France's Napoleon Bonaparte abdicates his throne, and Britain will soon start sending thousands of its best soldiers to fight in North America. The British newspapers demand vengeance on the Americans who had, according to the British, stabbed them in the back during the Napoleonic Wars.
- *July 5:* American troops, led by Gen. Winfield Scott and Gen. Jacob Brown, fight the British to a draw at the Battle of Chippewa, within earshot of Niagara Falls. The British commander, impressed by the American discipline, exclaims, "By God, those men are regulars!"
- *July 25:* Generals Scott and Brown fight the British to a draw at the Battle of Lundy's Lane, close to Niagara Falls.
- *August 8:* British and American delegates commence peace negotiations in Ghent, Belgium. As the weeks pass, some points are agreed to and others are postponed for future negotiations.
- *August 19:* Some 4,500 British troops, led by Gen. Robert Ross, disembark from ships at the village of Benedict, on the Patuxent River in Maryland, preparing to march on Washington, D.C., the next day.
- *August 24:* Ross's British troops decisively defeat U.S. militia units at the Battle of Bladensburg, just northeast of Washington, D.C.
- *August 24–25:* The British, led by General Ross, occupy Washington, D.C., for about 24 hours. Taking over the White House, the British

drink toasts to "Jemmy's [President James Madison] health" and then burn several homes and governmental buildings, including the White House and the Capitol. The British believe they are justified in this because Americans burned York (Toronto) in 1813. Taking with her the Gilbert Stuart painting of George Washington, First Lady Dolley Madison escapes the city just before the British arrive.

- *August 25:* The British troops head back to their ships on the Patuxent River.
- *August 27:* President Madison and nearly all of the government officials return to Washington, D.C. Madison vows to keep Washington as the nation's capital city.
- *August 31:* British general Sir George Prevost leads 10,000 crack British soldiers down from Montreal and across the border to Plattsburgh, New York, on the west side of Lake Champlain. Prevost commands the most formidable British army to invade during the war. He feels confident, too, because Capt. George Downie is moving down Lake Champlain with a small fleet.

British troops capture and burn Washington, D.C., August 24, 1814.
(National Archives, Still Pictures Branch, NWDNS-111-SC-96969)

This 1814 American cartoon mocks the British efforts to recover from its losses at the Battle of Lake Champlain, September 11, 1814. *(Library of Congress, Prints & Photographs Division [LC-USZ62-27679])*

- *September 11:* American commandant Thomas MacDonough wins the naval Battle of Lake Champlain over British captain George Downie. After the American naval victory, British general Prevost turns about and heads to Canada.
- *September 13–14:* A combination of U.S. Army and town militia units defend Baltimore, Maryland, from an attack by British land and sea forces. British general Robert Ross is killed early in the land fighting. Fort McHenry, at the entrance to the harbor, withstands a nighttime barrage of cannonballs and rocket fire. When morning comes, the American flag, 42 by 30 foot, still waves over Fort McHenry. Francis Scott Key, an American lawyer, aboard the British fleet to negotiate an exchange of prisoners, is moved to write a poem, "The Star Spangled Banner"; set to the tune of an English drinking song, it will become the U.S. national anthem in 1931.

- *November 7:* General Andrew Jackson captures Spanish-held Pensacola, Florida. Jackson claims that British ships were using the Spanish port, making it fair game for an American attack.
- *December 2:* After an exhausting forced march from Pensacola, General Jackson arrives in New Orleans and assumes command of all forces there. Jackson knows there is a British fleet in the Gulf of Mexico and suspects it has its eye on New Orleans.
- *December 15:* Many New Englanders have been feeling especially harmed by the war, and a number of prominent Federalists, opposed to Madison's polices, begin a secret convention in Hartford, Connecticut, to consider various proposals.
- *December 23:* British army and naval units come within eight miles of New Orleans before they are detected. They have achieved the element of surprise by crossing Lake Borgne, instead of coming up the Mississippi River.
- *December 23–24:* Learning that the British are so close, Jackson musters all available men and makes an attack on their position that evening. He exclaims: "By the Eternal! They shall not sleep on our soil." After a fierce nighttime engagement, the Americans pull back. They leave the British in possession of the field, but the element of surprise is gone, and the Americans have shown their ability to hit hard and hit fast.
- *December 24:* In Belgium, American and British diplomats sign the Treaty of Ghent. The treaty says virtually nothing about impressment, which had been the major reason for the war in the first place. All territory reverts to the nations that held it before the war began. Because of the normal travel time required, news of this treaty will not arrive in the United States for almost three weeks.

1815

- *January 1:* British general Sir Edward Pakenham begins a blistering artillery exchange between British and American lines just south of the city of New Orleans. Many of the U.S. cannons are manned by pirates from the group of Jean Lafitte. They have agreed to serve the American cause in return for an offer of amnesty for their former deeds.
- *January 5:* The Hartford Convention has rejected the proposal of secession but has decided on seeking seven amendments to the U.S.

Constitution. Three of the delegates set off for Washington to present their requests.

- *January 8:* The Battle of New Orleans begins at 8 A.M. General Pakenham leads a concerted British effort to dislodge the Americans from both sides of the canal that blocks the road to New Orleans. Fog clears just as the battle begins, and American sharpshooters from Kentucky, Tennessee, and elsewhere find their marks. British troops fall in great numbers, Pakenham is killed early on, and Gen. John Lambert gives up the contest within half an hour. The British suffer 192 killed, 1,265 wounded, and 484 missing. American losses are 13

Dressed in scarlet and white and advancing in close formation, British soldiers made easy targets for American snipers hidden in the woods in the Battle of New Orleans, January 8, 1815. *(National Archives, Still Pictures Branch, NWDNS-111-SC-90918)*

killed, 13 wounded, and 19 missing. It is one of the most one-sided battles ever fought between British and Americans; it is also one of the very last.

- *February 11:* The HMS *Favourite* enters New York Harbor, bringing copies of the Treaty of Ghent. Hearing of this, the delegates from the Hartford Convention choose not to present their "requests" to Congress.
- *February 17:* The U.S. Senate unanimously ratifies the Treaty of Ghent.
- *February 18:* President Madison announces that the war is officially ended.
- *February 20:* Unaware that the war is over, American captain Charles Stewart, aboard the USS *Constitution,* meets and defeats two smaller British ships off Madeira. One of the two prizes is recaptured during his home voyage, but on May 15 Stewart reaches New York Harbor, where he receives a hero's welcome and the thanks of Congress.

Results

During the course of the war, the United States suffered 2,260 men killed and another 4,505 wounded. At least 1,000 American civilians died during the war, mostly from Indian attacks in Ohio and Indiana. The U.S. Army executed 205 men during the war, most for desertion.

British losses are more difficult to document; they seldom released lists, but it is believed that their casualty figures were much like those of the Americans. This does not include the casualty losses for Canadian militiamen who served sporadically. American privateers also inflicted severe damage to British commerce, capturing as many as 2,000 British merchant vessels.

American Indian losses are even harder to document. It is possible that as many as 2,000 Indians were killed and that several times that many were displaced during the war. The loss of so many warriors was devastating to the Indian cause in the Ohio Valley area; they would never again be such a powerful force.

3

THE U.S.-
MEXICAN WAR

In 1821, Mexico won its independence from Spain. Just before this occurred, the Spanish government had agreed to let North Americans settle in the territory of New Spain known as Texas, which on the map drawn by the Adams-Onís Treaty of 1819 clearly belonged to Mexico. After Mexico threw off its Spanish rulers, it agreed to allow the North Americans into Texas so long as they agreed to abide by Spanish laws. Meanwhile, the Adams-Onís Treaty was reconfirmed by the United States as well as Mexico. Between 1820 and 1830, American settlers crossed the Sabine River into Texas in such numbers that by 1830 they outnumbered the Mexicans in Texas by about 20,000 to 3,000.

1830–1837

- In 1830, the Mexican federal government outlaws slavery and the importation of servant labor. Americans in Texas quietly defy the new law. In 1835, the Mexican government cracks down on individual states; one is Texas-Coahuilla. The Americans in Texas revolt and early in 1836 declare their independence. Mexican president Santa Anna, who considers himself a military genius, the "Napoleon of the West," marches north to subdue the Texans. Santa Anna captures the Alamo in San Antonio at great cost, then takes 300 prisoners at Goliad. Because he does not want the burden of feeding prisoners, Santa Anna has the 300 men shot in the back. Just as much as "Remember the Alamo," "Remember Goliad" becomes a rallying cry for Texans against Mexico. Santa Anna is completely defeated at the Battle of San Jacinto. Texan leader Sam Houston imposes peace terms, which include Texan independence. Santa Anna signs the treaty, but the Mexican federal government repudiates it, and Mexico refuses to accept that Texas has become an independent country, sometimes called the Lone Star Republic.

1837–1844

- Texas remains an independent country. Other countries, notably England and France, court it, but it remains separate and free. Several bills are introduced into the U.S. Congress for the annexation of Texas, but all of them fail to pass. Northern congressmen believe the addition of Texas would give too much voting power to the southern, slaveholding states. Mexico continues to seek reacquisition of Texas, but its two military expeditions to effect this are both failures. So is a Texan attempt to take more territory from Mexico. In the spring of 1844, U.S. president John Tyler orders U.S. Army units to the Louisiana border of Texas.

1845

- *January:* Mexican president Santa Anna is deposed. Gen. José Joaquín Herrera is made the new interim president of Mexico.
- *March 4:* James K. Polk takes the oath of office as the 11th U.S. president. His inauguration speech asserts the U.S. right to Oregon Territory and declares that negotiations for American annexation of Texas concern only Texas and the United States. In response, the Mexican ambassador soon leaves Washington, D.C.
- *May:* Mexican leader Santa Anna is exiled to Havana, Cuba, for life.
- *June 11:* President Polk, committed to making Texas a state, orders Gen. Zachary Taylor with a detachment of the U.S. Army to guard the border of southeastern Texas against an "invasion" by Mexico. Taylor leads his troops to the Nueces River, which the Mexicans now reluctantly recognize as the border between Mexico and Texas.
- *July:* In the July-August issue of the *United States Magazine and Democratic Review,* John L. O'Sullivan writes of the "Manifest Destiny" of the United States, to take the entire continent for the millions of Americans who will be born in the future.

- *September 16:* President Polk and his cabinet decide to send John Slidell to Mexico City with an offer to buy upper California and the Southwest for up to $30 million. Polk has already confided to Secretary of the Navy George Bancroft that he intends to obtain the California coast; in particular Polk wants the splendid harbors of Puget Sound, San Francisco, and San Diego.
- *December 16:* Amid rumors that the government of Mexico will indeed sell land to the United States, a military coup takes place. Herrera is overthrown.

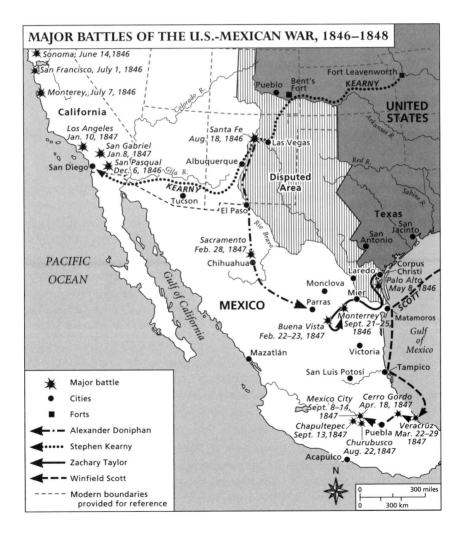

MAJOR BATTLES OF THE U.S.-MEXICAN WAR, 1846–1848

- *December 29:* President Polk signs the act that admits Texas to the Union.

1846

- *January 4:* Mariano Paredes y Arrillaga becomes the new Mexican president.
- *January 13:* Learning that the diplomatic mission of John Slidell has failed, President Polk sends orders to General Taylor to occupy the disputed area between the Nueces and Rio Grande Rivers. Whether this area is now the southern border of the United States or the northern border of Mexico remains open to dispute.
- *March 28:* General Taylor arrives at the north side of the Rio Grande. He sets up a camp called Fort Texas, near the Mexican town of Matamoros.
- *April 11:* Mexican general Pedro de Ampudia and 3,000 Mexican soldiers arrive at Matamoros on the south bank of the Rio Grande.
- *April 17:* Marine lieutenant Archibald Gillespie arrives at Monterey, California, with secret dispatches from President Polk for U.S. consul Thomas Larkin. Polk advises Larkin that the Americans in California should be ready to take and hold the area for the United States if a war breaks out.
- *April 23:* Mexican president Mariano Paredes announces a "defensive war" against the United States, based on the takeover of the land between the Nueces and Rio Grande Rivers.
- *April 24–25:* Mexican general Mariano Arista (who has just replaced Ampudia) sends 1,600 Mexican cavalrymen north of the Rio Grande. The Mexicans meet an American patrol of 56 men, all of whom are either killed or captured in this, the first skirmish between the two nations.
- *April 26:* General Taylor sends word to Washington, D.C., that "hostilities may now be considered as commenced."
- *May 8:* General Taylor wins the Battle of Palo Alto over the Mexicans led by General Arista. A key factor in the victory is the superiority of the American artillery. Taylor deploys "flying artillery," light guns pulled by horses. The Mexican gunpowder proves defective; many Mexican cannonballs hit the ground and bounce harmlessly to the U.S. lines.
- *May 9:* Lieutenant Gillespie reaches the explorers camp of John C. Frémont near Klamath Lake in present-day Oregon. Gillespie's mes-

This lithograph shows Gen. Zachary Taylor at the Battle of Resaca de la Palma, May 9, 1846. *(National Archives, Still Pictures Branch, NWDNS-111-SC-99035)*

sage is delivered orally, and the contents are not known, but the results were obvious. Frémont decamped, and by the end of May he and his men were in the vicinity of Sutter's Fort, near present-day Sacramento, California.

- *May 9:* Taylor's men win the Battle of Resaca de la Palma, just south of Palo Alto. At the battle's end, the Mexicans flee across the Rio Grande; many of them drown or are killed by American fire while they are in the water. Taylor does not pursue, but the battle leaves him in complete command of the north bank of the river.

- *May 11:* President Polk's request for a declaration of war is read in Congress. Polk argues that "Mexico has passed the boundary of the United States, has invaded our territory and shed American blood upon the American soil."

- *May 11–12:* Congress approves Polk's request. The declaration of war passes the House of Representatives, 174-14, and the Senate, 40-2. Some protest the action. Abraham Lincoln, elected to Congress in 1846, will introduce his "spot resolutions" in 1847. Lincoln will demand that Polk show on what exact spot Mexico shed American blood.

- *May 13:* Polk signs the War Bill that Congress has passed; it declares that "a state of war exists" with Mexico.
- *June 3:* Brig. Gen. Stephen Kearny receives secret orders. He is to march from Fort Leavenworth, Kansas, to Santa Fe, New Mexico, subdue the Mexican population there, and then march on to California. Kearny and his Army of the West depart on June 26.
- *June 10:* The U.S. Senate accepts the new boundary treaty with Britain concerning the Oregon country. Although Polk and others had demanded "Fifty-Four Forty or Fight," the new treaty draws the line between the United States and British Canada at the 49th parallel of longitude. The ships of both nations are allowed access to the Gulf of San Juan de Fuca. The agreement wards off any threat of war between Britain and the United States, thereby allowing President Polk to concentrate on Mexico.
- *June 14:* Americans in California capture the town of Sonoma. The Americans ride behind a flag that shows a bear and the Lone Star of Texas. Led by John C. Frémont, the Americans in California carry out what is known as the Bear Flag Revolt.
- *July 1:* Americans in California converge on the town of Yerba Buena (it will become San Francisco after the war is over).
- *July 4:* Frémont makes a speech in Yerba Buena to the effect that California is now an independent republic.
- *July 7:* U.S. commodore John Sloat sails into the harbor of Monterey, California, of which he takes possession.
- *July 9:* Comdr. John Sloat proclaims California a U.S. territory. For all practical purposes, the month-long "Bear Flag Republic" had come to an end.
- *July 23:* Comdr. Robert Stockton replaces Sloat as U.S. naval commander off the coast of California.
- *August 16:* Santa Anna steps ashore at Veracruz, Mexico. The beginning of the war found him in exile in Cuba. Santa Anna sends messages to President Polk, declaring that if he were allowed to return home and set up a new government, he would make peace with the United States. The U.S. blockade ships allow Santa Anna to reach Veracruz. Within weeks, he has declared he intends to continue the war.
- *August 17:* Frémont and marine lieutenant Archibald Gillespie enter and occupy Los Angeles.
- *September 19–24:* General Taylor's army besieges and captures the town of Monterrey, in northern Mexico.

- *September 25:* General Kearny leaves New Mexico, headed for California. He leaves behind Col. Sterling Price, whose orders are to occupy Santa Fe.
- *September 25:* Lieutenant Gillespie raises a flag of truce and hands Los Angeles over to the Mexicans who have threatened a cannonade.
- *October 6:* General Kearny meets the scout Kit Carson, who has been sent to guide Kearny into southern California.
- *November:* Colonel Doniphan leaves Santa Fe with 856 men and 315 wagons, headed for northern Mexico.
- *November 18:* President Polk formally appoints Gen. Winfield Scott commander of the U.S. force intended to land on the Mexican coast the following year. Polk has waited until now because he does not want to support the future political ambitions of either General Scott or Gen. Zachary Taylor.
- *December 6:* At San Pasqual, some 30 miles northeast of San Diego, California, Kearny's force of 100 suffers heavy casualties at the hands of a larger Mexican force, but the Mexicans then withdraw, fearing the arrival of U.S. reinforcements.

Leader of the so-called Ring-tailed Roarers, Alexander William Doniphan led key battles in 1847 but also gained a notorious reputation. *(Library of Congress, Prints & Photographs Division [LC-USZ62-109945])*

1847

- *January 8:* U.S. forces defeat the Mexicans at the San Gabriel River, 12 miles outside Los Angeles; although a minor engagement, U.S. forces now have a clear way to Los Angeles.
- *January 10:* American forces reenter Los Angeles. The revolt of the Californios (Mexicans in California) is over.
- *January 19:* A revolt breaks out against American rule in Taos, New Mexico. It has been an occupied town for three months, and the Mexicans rise up in fury, killing Governor Charles Bent and five other Americans.
- *January 28:* The advance units of the Mexican army leave San Luis Potosí, headed north. Santa Anna has assembled about 18,000 men, many of them raw conscripts. Santa Anna intends to surprise and crush the U.S. Army under General Taylor in northern Mexico.
- *February 3–4:* Col. Sterling Price subdues the Taos Revolt. One hundred fifty New Mexicans are killed in the fighting, and 15–30 are sentenced to death by firing squad.
- *February 21:* General Scott arrives at Lobos Island, halfway between Tampico and Veracruz on the east coast of Mexico. The island is the rendezvous point for Scott's army and naval forces.
- *February 22:* At Buena Vista, U.S. forces under General Taylor fight a large Mexican army led by Santa Anna. The battle rages throughout the afternoon and is touch and go most of the way. At one point, the American left flank crumbles under furious Mexican assaults; the flank is saved and then shored up by the heroic action of Missouri riflemen led by Col. Jefferson Davis, son-in-law of General Taylor. By nightfall, both armies are exhausted. The Mexicans pull out and retreat the next day; the Americans are too battle weary to give pursuit. Though the Americans lose 700 men dead or wounded, it is a decided victory for Taylor and his army: they remain in possession of northern Mexico for the rest of the war.
- *February 28:* Colonel Doniphan's column meets nearly 2,700 Mexican soldiers at Sacramento, Mexico. The U.S. artillery is superior, and Doniphan inflicts severe casualties on the Mexicans, with only slight losses to his force. Doniphan then enters and occupies the city of Chihuahua.
- *March 2:* General Scott's fleet leaves Isla Lobos and heads toward Veracruz.

The caption of this lithograph reads, "Col. Harney's brilliant charge at the Battle of Cerro Gordo," fought in April 1847. *(Library of Congress, Prints & Photographs Division [LC-USZ62-62226])*

- *March 9:* American commodore David Conner directs the landing of more than 7,000 men at a beach called Collado, south of Veracruz. It is the largest amphibious operation yet undertaken by American troops. Thousands more will come ashore in the next two weeks.
- *March 21:* The American bombardment of Veracruz begins.
- *March 28:* Both Veracruz and the fortress of San Juan de Ulua surrender to General Scott.
- *April 8:* General Scott sends the first units upcountry, beginning the 260-mile march to Mexico City. (Among the officer corps are Ulysses S. Grant and Robert E. Lee.) It is imperative to move inland, since the dreaded yellow fever (known then as *vomito negro*) season is about to commence along the coast.
- *April 17–18:* The Battle of Cerro Gordo is fought between Scott's Americans and a new Mexican army, put together by Santa Anna. The battle commences in a small way, on April 17. Overnight, American scouts and engineers haul guns around the Mexican left flank. The Americans strike both head on and from the left flank the next morning. The Mexican army is routed by 10 A.M.
- *May 15:* After light resistance from the Mexican forces, the U.S. Army takes Puebla, a large city on the road to Mexico City.

- *June 6:* General Scott sends seven regiments back to Veracruz, where they will be demobilized and sent home. They were 12-month recruits. With their departure, Scott is down to about 7,000 men, nearly all of whom are steady combat veterans.
- *August 7:* U.S. forces depart Puebla for Mexico City.
- *August 20:* General Scott's men, who have completed a complex maneuver to the south of Mexico City, fight the twin battles of Contreras and Churubusco with the Mexican defenders. The Battle of Contreras takes place at dawn; the surprised Mexicans are swiftly routed. The Battle of Churubusco is hard fought. The Mexicans defend a convent and the surrounding area; the battle lasts all afternoon. The Americans suffer 900 men killed, wounded, or missing; the Mexicans suffer about 2,500 such losses.
- *August 23–September 6:* An armistice is in effect within a 78-mile range of Mexico City. No hostilities occur during this time, but the U.S. mediator, Nicholas Trist, finds it impossible to make progress in talks between the two sides. On September 6, General Scott announces that the armistice has come to an end.

The Battle of Churubusco in August 1847 was a decisive victory for Gen. Winfield Scott. *(National Archives, Still Pictures Branch, NWDNS-111-SC-96986)*

- *September 8:* Scott's Americans make a frontal assault on Molino del Rey ("the King's Mill"), just south of Mexico City. The Mexicans resist fiercely, and the position is taken only after hand-to-hand combat. The Americans suffer 116 killed and 665 wounded; Mexican losses are much higher.
- *September 12–13:* Americans and Mexicans fight the battle for Chapultepec, which means "Hill of the Grasshoppers." Chapultepec is a citadel that houses the cadets of the Mexican military academy; it also commands the entrance to the western gates of Mexico City. General Scott begins the day with a cannonade of the Mexican position, followed by assaults led by Generals Twiggs and Pillow. Chapultepec falls in the morning of September 13. According to Mexican annals, a handful of teenage cadets chose to leap to their deaths from the walls rather than surrender. They are known as Los Niños Héroes ("the Heroic Children") in Mexican history.
- *September 14:* General Scott leads the U.S. forces into the main plaza of Mexico City. It is the first time an American army has taken the capital city of a foreign nation.
- *September 25–October 6:* Mexican army units besiege an American garrison in the town of Puebla. The Mexicans come close to success, but the siege is lifted on October 6. This is the last major combat action of the war.

1848

- *February 2:* Mexican commissioners sign the Treaty of Guadalupe Hidalgo. The United States is represented by Nicholas Trist. The United States gains the land known today as the American Southwest: all of Arizona, California, Nevada, New Mexico will emerge as states and parts will go to Colorado and Wyoming. The United States makes a token payment of $15 million to Mexico, which is shorn of one-third its territory. The United States also pays out another $38 million in claims made against Mexico.
- *February 28:* The U.S. Senate ratifies the Treaty of Guadalupe Hidalgo by a vote of 38-14, with four abstentions.
- *June 12:* The American flag is replaced by the Mexican flag in Mexico City.
- *November 7:* Zachary Taylor, the hero of Monterrey and of Buena Vista, is elected the 12th president of the United States.

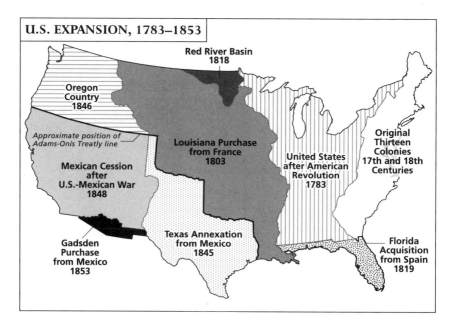

U.S. EXPANSION, 1783–1853

Red River Basin
1818

Oregon
Country
1846

Approximate position of
Adams-Onís Treatly line

Louisiana Purchase
from France
1803

United States
after American
Revolution
1783

Original
Thirteen
Colonies
17th and 18th
Centuries

Mexican Cession
after
U.S.-Mexican War
1848

Gadsden
Purchase
from Mexico
1853

Texas Annexation
from Mexico
1845

Florida
Acquisition
from Spain
1819

Results

Official U.S. casualty records indicate that 935 members of the regular army and 613 volunteers were killed in combat. Disease claimed a far higher number—4,714 members of the regular army and 6,256 of the volunteers. Mexican losses are much harder to determine. By using major battles as indicators, it has been estimated that as many as 15,000 Mexicans were killed or wounded in combat. The losses from disease may have been much higher but are unknown.

Long known in the United States as the Mexican War and in Mexico as the American Intervention, this conflict had long-reaching results. The United States obtained more than 500,000 square miles of territory which increased its size by 50 percent and reached what many advocates of Manifest Destiny considered its natural boundaries: the Pacific Ocean and the Rio Grande River. Most important for the future, the United States had become a two-ocean country, a fact that would lend it commercial and naval strength in the future.

The war was a disaster for Mexico. For a young country (its constitution was only 24 years old in 1848), to be beaten so decisively and to lose so much of its land was a calamity. Mexican politics continued to be turbulent through the 1850s and 1860s; only in 1867, when Benito Juárez became the first full-blooded Mexican Indian to take the presidency did the nation start to approach a measure of calm and good government.

4

THE CIVIL WAR

The treaty that ended the U.S.-Mexican War in 1848 brought a large new territory to the United States; there were demands from both sides to allow slavery or not allow slavery as parts of this territory became states. In September 1850, Congress approved a series of bills that collectively are known as the Compromise of 1850. Although these measures are intended to stave off the possibility of civil conflict, the nation becomes increasingly divided between those who favor the continuation of slavery and those who oppose the very existence of slavery. The division does not always follow a clear North-South line, but as the decade continues, the division between North and South becomes increasingly rigid. Events such as the publication of *Uncle Tom's Cabin* in 1852, the Dred Scott decision by the Supreme Court in 1857, and John Brown's raid on Harpers Ferry in 1859 increase the tension.

1860

- *February 27:* Mathew Brady photographs Abraham Lincoln just before he is to deliver an important speech at Cooper Union, New York. Lincoln will later attribute his election victory to the speech and Brady's photograph, which is widely reproduced. Brady and his crew of photographers will later capture the texture of the war with amazing realism.
- *April 23:* The Democratic Party convention meets in Charleston, South Carolina. The party cannot agree on a platform—much less a candidate—and the convention adjourns on May 3. The Demo-

John Brown, leader of the antislavery uprising at Harpers Ferry, Virginia, rides his own coffin to his execution, December 2, 1859. Brown's death transforms him from renegade to martyr in the eyes of some. *(Library of Congress, Prints & Photographs Division [LC-USZ62-79479])*

cratic Party then splits into two groups: Northern and Southern Democrats.

- *May 16:* On the third ballot, the Republican Party nominates Abraham Lincoln of Illinois as its presidential candidate. The Democrats split over slavery and other issues. Northern Democrats will nominate Stephen Douglas of Illinois (he and Lincoln had clashed in the celebrated debates of 1858); the Southern Democrats will nominate John C. Breckinridge. Meanwhile, a newly formed fourth party, the Constitution Union Party, has nominated John Bell as its candidate.
- *November 6:* Lincoln wins the four-way race for president. Although he wins handily in the Electoral College—180 votes out of 303—he has only 40 percent of the popular vote; all his electoral votes and most of his popular votes are from the North.

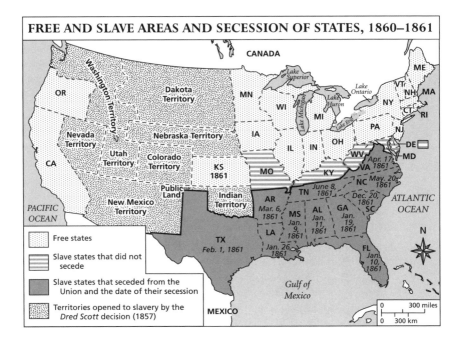

FREE AND SLAVE AREAS AND SECESSION OF STATES, 1860–1861

- *December 20:* South Carolina secedes from the Union. Leaders of the special state convention cite the long-held belief in states' rights, particularly the right of states to depart from the Union if that union oppresses them. The declaration ends with these words: "the union now subsisting between South Carolina and the other States, under the name of the 'United States of America,' is hereby dissolved."
- *December 26:* Maj. Robert Anderson, commander of Fort Moultrie in the harbor of Charleston, South Carolina, shifts his garrison to the stronger and better armed Fort Sumter.

1861

- *January 5–9:* The federal government sends a merchant ship, the *Star of the West,* with 250 U.S. Army troops, to support the troops in Charleston Harbor. When the South Carolina forces fire on the ship as it enters the harbor, it turns back to New York.
- *January 9:* Mississippi secedes from the Union.
- *January 10:* Florida secedes from the Union.
- *January 11:* Alabama secedes from the Union.

THE CIVIL WAR

- *January 19:* Georgia secedes from the Union.
- *January 26:* Louisiana secedes from the Union.
- *January 29:* Kansas enters the Union as the 34th state.
- *February 1:* Texas declares secession.
- *February 5:* President James Buchanan informs South Carolina that under no circumstances will Fort Sumter be yielded.
- *February 18:* Jefferson Davis takes the oath of office as president of the new Confederate States of America. The convention is held in Montgomery, Alabama, but the capital will soon be shifted to Richmond, Virginia. In his inaugural speech, Davis extols the virtues of the southern states, particularly their emphasis on local government.

Lincoln is sworn in as president at the U.S. Capitol, March 4, 1861. By this time, seven Southern states have already seceded from the Union (ultimately four more will do so) and Jefferson Davis has been president of the new Confederate States of America for six weeks. *(Library of Congress, Prints & Photographs Division [LC-USZ62-48564])*

- *February 23:* Abraham Lincoln, the president-elect, arrives in Washington, D.C. The last part of his trip is undertaken in secrecy, to prevent possible assassination attempts. Lincoln is not well known or appreciated in Washington. He is seen as a political outsider, a compromiser who has made his way to the top through vacillation and good fortune.
- *March 4:* Lincoln takes the presidential oath of office. In his inaugural speech, Lincoln emphasizes that he, and the federal government, will not push war on the southern states. If war comes, it will be of their choosing.
- *March 11:* The new Confederate Congress adopts a permanent constitution. It provides for a president, a vice president, and a unicameral legislature. There is also a strong emphasis on state's rights, which will make the work of the new government difficult in the coming war.
- *March 29:* Having vacillated for some weeks, Lincoln announces that he intends to send a force to resupply Fort Sumter. Lincoln knows that, lacking supplies, the fort will fall, but he is loath to give the South an excuse to begin armed conflict.
- *April:* Gen. Winfield Scott, military adviser to Lincoln, presents what will become known as his "Anaconda Plan" to the president. Since Lincoln has made it clear that his goal will never be to annihilate the South but to bring it back into the Union, the Anaconda Plan calls for a slow strangulation of the Confederacy by blockading the Southern coastline and eventually gaining control of the Mississippi. Meanwhile, Federal land armies will move against Confederate forces at appropriate locations in the east and west.
- *April 12:* After Major Anderson rejected the Confederate demand on April 11 that he surrender Fort Sumter, Confederate guns open fire on the fort. The first Confederate cannon is reportedly trained by Gen. Pierre Beauregard. The first Union cannon is supposedly commanded by Maj. Abner Doubleday (who some 47 years later would be wrongly credited with having invented baseball).
- *April 13:* After enduring a 34-hour bombardment, Major Anderson and the garrison surrender. The Civil War has begun.
- *April 15:* Lincoln issues a call for 75,000 volunteer soldiers. Lincoln declines to call the conflict a war, naming it an "insurrection." This wording will give him greater powers as president and commander-in-chief.

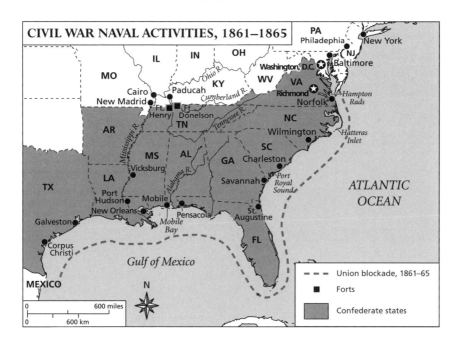

CIVIL WAR NAVAL ACTIVITIES, 1861–1865

- *April 17:* Virginia secedes from the Union.
- *April 18:* Through emissaries of Lincoln, Robert E. Lee is offered the command of the federal army. Lee, who had been a hero in the U.S.-Mexican War, instead resigns his U.S. commission and chooses to side with his home state.
- *April 19:* Ulysses Grant, who has been working in his father's leather-goods store in Galena, Illinois, writes to his father-in-law: "all party distinctions should be lost sight of, and every true patriot be for maintaining the integrity of the glorious old Stars and Stripes, the Constitution and the Union.
- *April 27:* Lincoln suspends the writ of habeas corpus, the constitutional right which all accused persons have to contest their detention, in an area extending from Philadelphia to Washington, D.C. Authority to extend this perimeter is given to Gen. Winfield Scott.
- *April 29:* The lower house of the Maryland legislature rejects a measure for secession by a vote of 53-13. It is a serious blow to the Confederate cause, as Confederate planners had hoped to be able to surround the capital district of Washington.

- *May 6:* Jefferson Davis approves the Confederate Congress bill declaring a state of war with the United States. Arkansas secedes from the Union.
- *May 20:* North Carolina secedes from the Union.
- *May 21:* Union troops cross the Potomac River and occupy Alexandria, Virginia. When 24-year-old Union colonel Elmer Ellsworth attempts to take down a Confederate flag atop a hotel, he is shot and killed by hotelkeeper James Jackson. Both Ellsworth and Jackson soon are regarded as heroes by their respective regions, North and South.
- *June 3:* Union general George B. McClellan routs a small Confederate force at Philippi, in what will later become the state of West Virginia.
- *June 8:* Tennessee is the 11th and last state to secede from the Union.
- *June 9:* Lincoln approves the creation of the U.S. Sanitary Commission, which will have authority over all medical and nursing units.
- *June 9:* Mary Ann Bickerdyke arrives from Ohio at a Union army camp at Cairo, Illinois. That same day she begins what will be a four-year occupation of cleaning, nursing, and feeding sick Union soldiers. By 1863 she will be known as Mother Ann Bickerdyke.
- *June 10:* Dorothea Dix, who has already made a name and career as champion for the mentally ill, is appointed superintendent of all Union army nurses. The only other person who was considered is Elizabeth Blackwell, the first female physician in modern times.
- *June 10:* Confederate forces repulse a Union attack on Big Bethel, Virginia, near the Union stronghold of Fort Monroe.
- *June 30:* The CSS *Sumter* slips the Union blockade off New Orleans. Commander Raphael Semmes will later abandon his ship at Gibraltar, having taken 18 Union prizes in a six-month cruise.
- *June 28:* Having been appointed colonel of a group of Illinois volunteers, Ulysses Grant now takes his unit into Federal service as the Twenty-First Illinois Volunteers.
- *July 11–13:* Union forces defeat Confederates at Rich Mountain, present-day West Virginia, and Carrick's Ford, northwestern Virginia.
- *July 21:* The First Battle of Bull Run (known to the Confederates as First Manassas) is the first collision between major forces. Union general Irwin McDowell takes the offense but is thwarted. A group of Virginia infantry under Thomas Jackson stand so firm that a phrase is coined: "There stands Jackson, standing like a stone wall." The Confederates then take the offense and chase the Federal troops off the

The Union's Anaconda Plan constricted delivery of needed goods to the Confederate states by blockading Southern ports. Many merchant boats risked slipping the blockade, however, because profits were extraordinary. The steamer *Hudson,* shown here, was the first blockade runner captured. *(National Archives, Still Pictures Branch, NWDNS-111-B-4819)*

field; their disorganized retreat to Washington shocks the North. The Confederates suffer 1,982 men killed, wounded, or missing; the Federals lose 2,896. One witness to the battle and its aftermath is an impetuous government clerk from Massachusetts, Clara Barton. Soon after the battle she begins to organize an independent medical response team. By the summer of 1862, she and a small group of friends will be delivering supplies by mule teams.

- *July 27:* Gen. George B. McClellan replaces McDowell as commander of the Union forces in the East. McClellan will rename his troops the Army of the Potomac.
- *July 27:* Confederate forces capture 700 Union troops in St. Augustine Springs, New Mexico.
- *September 10–15:* In his first campaign, Gen. Robert E. Lee fails to defeat the union forces at Cheat Mountain, present-day West Virginia.

- *August 2:* Lincoln signs an income tax measure, the first ever in U.S. history. It provides for a 3 percent tax on incomes exceeding $800.
- *August 10:* At Wilson's Creek, Missouri, Union general Nathaniel Lyon is killed but the Federals hold off three Confederate attacks before withdrawing.
- *Late October:* To Lincoln's annoyance, McClellan orders the Army of the Potomac into winter quarters.
- *November 1:* Winfield Scott, hero of the Mexican War, officially retires. Lincoln and all the members of the presidential cabinet visit the ailing Scott at his Washington home to offer their congratulations on the conclusion of his remarkable career. Gen. George McClellan replaces him as commander of the Union armies.
- *November 1–7:* Union general Ulysses S. Grant moves south from Cairo, Illinois, and threatens the Confederates at Columbus, under Gen. Leonidas Polk. On November 7, Grant's forces rout the Confederates at Belmont, Missouri, but his men stop to loot the abandoned camp and are then forced to retreat.
- *November 6:* The voters of the Confederacy choose Jefferson Davis and Alexander Stephens (who have until now held provisional posts) as the president and vice president for six-year terms.
- *November 7:* Union soldiers and naval units work in unison to capture Forts Walker and Beauregard, which guard Port Royal Sound, South Carolina.
- *November 8:* Capt. Charles Wilkes of the USS *San Jacinto* stops the British mail ship *Trent* and removes two Confederate commissioners who are headed for England.
- *November 27:* News of the seizure of the two commissioners reaches Great Britain. Although the British public had, until now, favored the Union, an intense outcry occurs and many British people call for an apology or war with the Union.
- *December:* Great Britain prepares to rush 20,000 soldiers to defend Canada in the event of a U.S. invasion.
- *December 5:* Prince Albert, the Consort of Queen Victoria, amends a British diplomatic note to Secretary of State William Seward. The new softer tone allows Seward to back down gracefully, and the Trent Affair heads toward a peaceful conclusion.
- *December 9–10:* The U.S. Congress establishes the Joint Committee on the Conduct of the War. The 15-man committee will later have great authority.

- *December 30:* The United States releases the two Confederate commissioners to Lord Lyons, the British minister in Washington, D.C.

1862

- *January 13:* Lincoln appoints Edwin Stanton, a former U.S. attorney general, as the new secretary of war. The Senate confirms the appointment on January 15.
- *February 5–6:* General Ulysses Grant captures Fort Henry on the Tennessee River. Most of the Confederate garrison escapes and marches 12 miles overland to Fort Donelson on the Cumberland River.
- *February 12:* Grant leaves Fort Henry and heads toward Fort Donelson.
- *February 14–15:* Union gunboats bombard Fort Donelson. The Union boats take many hits from the shore defenses, and Grant decides to make a formal siege. The fort is commanded by Gen. Simon Buckner, a comrade-in-arms of Grant during the Mexican War.
- *February 16:* General Buckner asks for terms of surrender from Grant and receives this answer: "No terms except an unconditional and immediate surrender can be accepted. I propose to move immediately on your works." Thirteen thousand troops surrender in what is the largest Union victory so far in the war. Grant soon becomes known as "Unconditional Surrender" Grant.
- *March 7–8:* At Pea Ridge, in northern Arkansas, Federal forces defeat the Confederates. Fighting alongside the latter were several thousand Indians led by Confederate Gen. Stand Watie, himself a Cherokee.
- *March 8:* The CSS *Virginia* (previously a U.S. Navy ship, the *Merrimack*) steams out of Norfolk Harbor and meets Union ships. One Union ship is sunk, another goes aground, and it is shown that wooden ships are no match for this new ironclad.
- *March 9:* The first battle between ironclad ships takes place off the Virginia coast. The CSS *Virginia* meets the USS *Monitor* in a classic battle. The *Virginia* towers over the *Monitor,* but the shooting battle is a draw. The perseverance of the *Monitor,* however, ensures that the Confederates will not destroy the wooden ships of the U.S. Navy in that area.
- *March 14:* Union forces under Gen. Ambrose Burnside take New Berne, North Carolina. This is part of the Anaconda Plan.

Union forces at Yorktown, Virginia, May 1862. Gen. George McClellan moved the Army of the Potomac deliberately in the Peninsular Campaign to capture the Confederate capital of Richmond, Virginia. By the time that Federals finally attacked Yorktown, its Confederate defenders had secretly fled. *(National Archives, Still Pictures Branch, NWDNS-111-B-82.)*

- *March 17:* General McClellan moves 12 divisions of the Army of the Potomac by water to Fort Monroe, at the tip of the James Peninsula, Virginia. About 110,000 troops are moved in this remarkable amphibious operation. Only about 50,000 Confederates stand between him and Richmond, but McClellan, a cautious commander, decides to move forward slowly.

- *March 28:* Union forces win the Battle of Pigeon's Ranch near Santa Fe, New Mexico. The tide of Southern success in New Mexico is reversed.
- *April 6–7:* General Grant's Union forces are surprised by Confederates led by Gen. Albert Johnston at the Battle of Shiloh, southwestern Tennessee. Because of the location, this battle features many small conflicts between neighbors and even relatives. The Confederates do well on the first day; they break the Union line in several places, but a core of resistance by Gen. Benjamin Prentiss's division holds firm. Johnston dies in the fighting, and General Beauregard takes over. Beauregard later writes, "I thought I had General Grant just where I wanted him and could finish him up in the morning." Instead, it is Grant who counterattacks on the morning of April 7. By mid-afternoon the Confederates are in full retreat. In terms of casualties the battle is a standoff, but it is also a moral victory for the Union. President Lincoln later hears sharp criticisms of Grant for being surprised on the morning of April 6. Lincoln responds, "I can't spare this man, he fights."

Commodore Farragut's squadron and Captain Porter's mortar fleet enter the Mississippi River, April 18, 1862. A week later, they compel the surrender of New Orleans. *(Library of Congress, Prints & Photographs Division [LC-USZ62-91432])*

- *April 16:* President Jefferson Davis approves an act of the Confederate Congress providing for conscription, the first ever seen in North America. Planters or overseers on plantations with more than 20 slaves are exempted from service.
- *April 18:* Union admiral David Glasgow Farragut brings his fleet across the sandbars and into the mouth of the Mississippi River. Only 75 miles separate him from New Orleans.
- *April 18–24:* Farragut's fleet exchanges cannon fire with Confederate Forts Jackson and St. Philip on the lower Mississippi River. On the night of April 24, Farragut carries out a daring nighttime pass of the defenses of the forts.
- *April 25:* New Orleans, helpless because of Farragut's pass of the forts, surrenders.
- *April 26:* Farragut enters and occupies New Orleans. The Crescent City, as New Orleans is known, has fallen faster and more easily than anyone might have expected.
- *April 29–May 30:* Following the battle at Shiloh, Federal troops now led by Gen. Henry Halleck pursue the Confederates until they are forced to abandon their stronghold in Corinth, Mississippi.
- *May 5:* Advance units of the Army of the Potomac clash with Confederates at the Battle of Williamsburg, fought near the former capital of colonial Virginia.
- *May 11:* Trapped in Norfolk, Virginia, by the advancing troops of General McClellan, the CSS *Merrimack* is blown up by its crew.
- *May 13:* Stonewall Jackson wins the Battle of McDowell in his campaign in the Shenandoah Valley. Jackson, who is outnumbered three to one, was expected to remain on the defensive, but he pursues the opposite tack, in order to draw away men and supplies from the Union move on Richmond.
- *May 20:* Lincoln signs the Homestead Act. It provides for settlers to receive the title to up to 160 acres of land from the public domain once they have settled on it and made improvements for five years.
- *May 23:* Stonewall Jackson wins the Battle of Front Royal in the Shenandoah Valley.
- *May 25:* Stonewall Jackson wins the Battle of Winchester in the Shenandoah Valley.
- *June 1:* Gen. Robert E. Lee, who has been stationed in Richmond advising President Jefferson Davis, replaces the wounded General Johnston as commander of the Army of Northern Virginia.

- *June 8–9:* Stonewall Jackson wins twin victories at Cross Keys and Port Republic in his remarkable Shenandoah Valley campaign. In the past 38 days, Jackson and his men have marched more than 400 miles and fought five battles. By now, Jackson's men are convinced he is the greatest military leader of the age, and they will be ready to follow him into any sort of future danger.
- *June 25–July 1:* The Battles of the Seven Days are fought around the eastern perimeter of Richmond, Virginia. (The most important are Oak Grove, Mechanicsville, Gaines's Mill, White Oak Swamp, and Malvern Hill.) General Lee makes numerous attacks, which cost him at least as many casualties as he inflicts. Just the same, General McClellan fears he is outnumbered, and he makes plans to retreat down the James Peninsula.
- *July 1:* Lincoln signs the act that provides for a transcontinental railroad to be built by the Union Pacific and Central Pacific companies.
- *July 2:* Lincoln signs the Morrill Land Act. Introduced by Vermont senator Justin Morrill, the act provides for the establishment of agricultural and technical colleges in all the states; this leads eventually to institutions that become the great state universities of the 20th century.
- *July 4–31:* Confederate general John Hunt Morgan leads a cavalry force of some 800 on a daring raid from Tennessee into Kentucky. They destroy various supply depots and capture some 1,200 Federals.
- *July 6–27:* While Morgan is leading his raid, Confederate general Nathan Bedford Forrest leads his cavalry unit on an equally daring series of raids on Union forces and depots in Tennessee. He destroys railroad bridges and causes Federal generals to divert large numbers of their forces.
- *July 11:* Disappointed at McClellan's lack of aggressiveness, Lincoln appoints Henry Halleck as general in chief of all Union forces. Although Halleck is a first-class organizer, he will turn out no better than McClellan when it comes to field operations.
- *August 14:* Frederick Douglass, an escaped slave who has become the outstanding spokesperson for his fellow African Americans, visits Lincoln in the White House. Douglass urges Lincoln to broaden the war effort, to put it in a moral basis by insisting upon the abolition of slavery. Douglass comes away from the meeting with the belief that Lincoln will increase his efforts to shift the focus toward the issue of slavery.

- *August 22:* The War Department announces that it will recruit blacks, including freed slaves, to serve in the Union army.
- *August 29:* In the Second Battle of Bull Run (Second Manassas), Lee soundly defeats Union general John Pope and his Army of Virginia. Lee now thinks this is the time to cross into Union territory and win a major battle on Northern soil. This is one of the perennial hopes of the Confederate high command; they believe such a victory might persuade Britain, France, or both to come into the war as a Confederate ally.
- *September 4:* Lee's Army of Northern Virginia crosses the Potomac River into Maryland. Hoping to stir up sympathizers to their cause, the Confederates sing, "Maryland, my Maryland." The Confederates are led by that now-remarkable combination of Lee and Stonewall Jackson. Lee is the consummate strategist who thinks of ways to outfox the enemy; Jackson is the consummate man of action who leads his columns in the bold maneuvers conceived by Lee.
- *September 13:* General McClellan receives a copy of Lee's dispatches, which were found by two soldiers from the twenty-seventh Indiana. Gleeful, McClellan says, "Here is a paper with which if I cannot whip Bobbie Lee, I will be willing to go home."
- *September 14–16:* McClellan's forces converge more rapidly than Lee's, but McClellan's traditional caution prevents him from attacking quickly and administering a crippling blow.
- *September 17:* Lee and McClellan's armies clash at Antietam, Maryland, just one mile from the Potomac River. The advantage of numbers is very much with the Union, but Lee has chosen the ground well, and fights a grueling defensive battle. The conflict breaks into three sections, each one marked by a landmark: a church, a road, and a bridge. The Union takes and holds the offensive all day long. When nightfall comes, Lee's men are near a complete collapse, but the punishing results persuade McClellan not to renew the contest the next day. The dead for both sides are estimated to total at least 4,800, with another 1,700 wounded; Antietam becomes known as the bloodiest single day of the war, and it remains so in U.S. history.
- *September 19:* In the early morning hours, Lee and the Army of Northern Virginia cross the Potomac to reach safety. They have survived to fight again another day.
- *September 23:* Lincoln's draft of the Emancipation Proclamation is published in Northern newspapers. The standoff battle of Antietam

was not a true victory, but it gave Lincoln the momentum he believed he needed in order to issue the proclamation. Although it is not all-inclusive (in fact it frees only the slaves who are in the states currently in rebellion), the proclamation is hailed by Frederick Douglass and others as a bold step forward.

- *September 24:* Lincoln suspends habeas corpus and provides for military trials of all "Rebels and Insurgents." Anyone suspected of disloyalty can be held and imprisoned without having to show just cause. Although Lincoln will be criticized for this, Jefferson Davis has also suspended habeas corpus.

- *September 27:* Gen. Benjamin Butler, the military governor of occupied New Orleans, musters in the First Louisiana Native Guards. They are the first regiment of free blacks.

- *October 3–4:* Confederate general Braxton Bragg attacks Union general Buell at Corinth, Mississippi. The Confederates are driven off, but Buell fails to pursue.

- *October 8:* At Perryville, Kentucky, a recently named brigadier general, Philip Sheridan, distinguishes himself by repulsing a strong Confederate attack and then ordering a counterattack.

- *November 7:* Lincoln replaces George McClellan with Gen. Ambrose Burnside. The new leader soon reorganizes the Army of the Potomac into three "Grand Divisions," each of which has two army corps.

- *December 2:* Harriet Beecher Stowe, author of the best-selling anti-slavery novel *Uncle Tom's Cabin,* and her sister are taken to the White House by Senator and Mrs. Henry Wilson of Massachusetts. Reports have circulated ever since that Lincoln greeted Stowe with, "So you're the little woman who started this great big war!" but no verification can be found in Stowe's diary or letters.

- *December 13:* The Battle of Fredericksburg is a complete disaster for General Burnside and the Army of the Potomac. The Federal attacks across the river result in nearly 7,000 men dead, wounded, or missing. Lee, watching from the opposite bank, is heard to say: "It is well that war is so terrible, for otherwise we should grow too fond of it."

- *December 28–29:* Gen. William Tecumseh Sherman launches attacks on Chickasaw Bayou in preparation for a greater attack on Vicksburg, Mississippi. The Federals are repulsed with more than 1,700 casualties.

- *December 31–January 3, 1862:* The Battle of Stones River (also known as Murfreesboro) takes place in Tennessee. The Federals under

Federal bombardment ruined the city of Fredericksburg, Virginia; well-placed Confederate volleys at the ensuing battle of Fredericksburg, December 13, 1862, rend through line after line of Federal infantry. *(National Archives, Still Pictures Branch, NWDNS-111-B-131)*

Gen. William Rosecrans turn back the Confederates under Gen. Braxton Bragg; after regrouping on New Year's Day, they rejoin battle and again the Confederates are repulsed.

1863

- *January 1:* Lincoln's Emancipation Proclamation takes effect. The president has consciously planned the wording so that slaves in the states then in rebellion were freed. It says nothing about the slaves in the border states or other Confederate areas already conquered by the Federals.
- *January 26:* Lincoln dismisses General Burnside and makes General Joseph ("Fighting Joe") Hooker the new leader of the Army of the Potomac.
- *March 3:* Lincoln signs the federal conscription law, first in the nation's history. Designed to provide 300,000 soldiers, the law has many loopholes. Records show that 86,724 men paid the commutation fee of $300; that another 117,986 hired a substitute (presumably for less than $300), and that only 50,663 men are actually drafted that year.

- *April 2:* There is a bread riot in Richmond, Virginia. Confederate president Jefferson Davis appears before the rioters and manages to soothe their anger.
- *April 16–22:* Union admiral David Porter, having failed at an attempt in March to aid Grant in his plan to take Vicksburg, manages to get past the Confederate batteries at Vicksburg with 22 gunboats, transport, and supply barges. Porter's fleet is then able to transport Grant's troops across to the east bank of the Mississippi, where they will soon commence a land campaign.
- *April 27:* General Hooker leads the Army of the Potomac out of camp, headed for the Rappahannock Ford. Hooker has welded the 120,000-man army into a powerful fighting force. Some of Hooker's critics have suggested he intends to become a military dictator in the future. In a letter to Hooker, Lincoln writes, "What I now ask of you is military success, and I will risk the dictatorship."
- *April 30:* Grant moves out of camp and crosses to the west side of the Mississippi River. He is now determined to capture Vicksburg, Mississippi, and thereby cut the Confederacy in half. Grant has designed a bold attack that will denude Vicksburg of some of its natural defenses. He will cross the river again and attack Vicksburg from the south and east, rather than from the north.
- *May 1–2:* General Hooker and the Army of the Potomac clash with General Lee and the army of Northern Virginia at Chancellorsville. Although outnumbered about 110,000 to 70,000, Lee chooses to divide his forces. Stonewall Jackson leads 20,000 men on a dramatic 12-mile flanking movement around the Union left on the morning of May 2. Jackson attacks at 6 P.M., and the Union lines give way. Hooker has been out of commission since noon when a cannon ball hit the chimney of the house where he has his headquarters; lacking its leader, the Union army becomes confused and demoralized. The Confederates score one of their greatest victories. The Union suffers 17,287 casualties; the Confederates 12,821. The magnitude of the Confederate victory is overshadowed by their greatest loss. Late that evening, Stonewall Jackson is mistakenly shot by a Confederate guard as he returns from a reconnaissance of the Union lines. Jackson's left arm is amputated in an attempt to save his life.
- *May 10:* Stonewall Jackson dies of the wound he suffered at Chancellorsville. Many Confederates will later say that half the spirit of the Army of Northern Virginia departed with Jackson.

- *May 14:* Grant enters Jackson, the capital of Mississippi.
- *May 16:* Grant defeats General Pemberton at Champion's Hill, Mississippi.
- *May 17:* Grant routs Pemberton at Big Black River. Pemberton falls back to the defenses of Vicksburg.
- *May 19:* Grant tries a head-on assault on Stockade Redan, part of Vicksburg's defenses. The Union troops are repulsed and suffer 3,000 killed, wounded, or missing.
- *May 23:* General Grant begins the formal siege of Vicksburg.
- *June 3:* Lee sends his men out of their camp at Fredericksburg, headed north. He is still intent on winning a victory on Northern soil.
- *June 20:* The new state of West Virginia enters the Union.
- *June 28:* As Lee's forces are moving toward Pennsylvania, Union general Joseph Hooker asks to be relieved of command of the defending forces because he feels his strategy has been undermined by Gen. Henry Halleck. Lincoln gives command to Gen. George Meade.
- *July 1:* Union and Confederate forces collide at Gettysburg, Pennsylvania. The encounter begins because Confederate soldiers are looking for shoes—a good indication of the outstretched Confederate supply lines. The Union troops are marching north; the Confederate troops are marching south. In the afternoon, the Confederates push the Union troops out of the town, but find the Union forces in an excellent defensive position, drawn up in a horseshoe formation. Culp's Hill is on the east side; Big and Little Round Tops are on the left west side; and Cemetery Ridge is in the center. Both Lee and Meade are actually drawn into a battle sooner and at a locale that neither had envisioned. Only the fact that the Union soldiers have the superior battleground positions saves them from a possibly disastrous defeat. The Union artillery on Cemetery Hill finally convinces the Confederates to stop, but the Union forces have suffered heavy casualties.
- *July 2:* Confederate and Union troops continue to arrive all morning. At breakfast, Lee announces his plan to crack the left wing of the horseshoe that is the Union position. Gen. James Longstreet objects, pointing out the strength of the Union positions, but Lee insists. Yet even he realizes that he is at some disadvantage because his cavalry under Gen. Jeb Stuart has been out of touch for a week now and so he lacks information about the disposition of the federal forces. Preliminary attacks during the morning and early afternoon meet determined Union resistance. The full battle only commences about 4 P.M.,

as the Confederates attempt to take the Round Tops. They do take Big Round Top but they are thwarted in their attack on Little Round Top by the heroic action of the Eleventh Maine Regiment, commanded by Col. Joshua Chamberlain. When his ammunition runs out, Chamberlain orders a bayonet charge downhill. The suddenness of the attack confounds the Confederates, who fall back in confusion. The battle's second day ends with the two sides in roughly the same positions they began.

- *July 3:* Acting against the advice of General Longstreet and others, Lee decides on a third and final attack, this one at the heart of the Union position on Cemetery Ridge. The Confederates open a fierce artillery bombardment to soften up the Northern position; General Meade senses the impending danger and shifts men to the central location. Starting about 2 P.M., some 14,000 Confederate infantry are organized by General Longstreet, but it is one of the division leaders, Gen. George Pickett, whose name will forever be attached to what follows. As the Confederates move across about a half-mile of open field, Union troops on Cemetery Ridge begin to fire artillery down on

Amputation being performed in a hospital tent at Gettysburg. Amputation was the accepted treatment for gangrene, and arms and legs were routinely amputated even when wounds were minor. *(National Archives, Still Pictures Branch, NWDNS-111-79-T-2265)*

them; as the Confederates come closer and closer, the Union troops let loose a steady barrage of rifle fire as well as artillery. Union soldiers call down the hill, "Fredericksburg!" remembering the blood they had spilled in December 1862. The attack is a complete disaster. Within this one hour, the Confederates have suffered about 7,000 men killed, wounded, or missing. Lee meets the surviving members of Pickett's division with the words, "It's my fault, it's all my fault." It is the worst defeat of his life. In the attack on Cemetery Ridge, Lee committed the errors that he usually was so adept at luring Union commanders into. It is possible that his attack might have had a better chance of success had Jeb Stuart arrived at the Federal rear with his cavalry, but he was stopped by Federal cavalry led by the youngest general in the Union army, 23-year-old George Armstrong Custer.

- *July 4:* Lee begins to lead the Army of Northern Virginia away from Gettysburg. Meade and the Army of the Potomac do not pursue.
- *July 4:* Gen. John Pemberton surrenders the fortress of Vicksburg to General Grant. The siege had reduced the Confederates to the extremity of eating rats. Grant's victory, while less sensational than Gettysburg, means that the Confederacy is effectively split in two: No supplies or reinforcements can travel from Texas to the other Confederate States, or vice versa. Lincoln recognizes the importance of Vicksburg. In a letter written to James Conkling in late August, Lincoln comments, "The Father of Waters again goes unvexed to the sea."
- *July 9:* Port Hudson, Louisiana, surrenders to Federal forces.
- *July 10–18:* Union naval and land forces move on Morris Island, in the harbor of Charleston, South Carolina. A direct assault on Confederate Fort Wagner fails on July 11, but a second attempt, on July 18, succeeds. The Massachusetts Fifty-fourth Regiment, composed entirely of African-American soldiers, with white officers, earns laurels for its bravery in the assault. Today the regiment is commemorated by a monument in Boston by Augustus Saint-Gaudens.
- *July 11:* Government officials draw the first names for the draft in New York City.
- *July 13–16:* Riots and looting take place in New York City in response to the draft. Many of the rioters are recent immigrants from Ireland, who resent having to fight what they call a "white man's war." The Seventh New York Infantry has to be called in to bring an end to three days of violence: One hundred nineteen people are dead and 306 are injured.

This memorial in Boston honors the daring charge on Fort Wagner, South Carolina, by the Fifty-fourth Massachusetts, a unit consisting entirely of black soldiers under white officers led by Robert Gould Shaw. The action demonstrated African Americans' courage and capability under fire, prompting more recruitment of blacks in the Union army. *(Library of Congress, Prints & Photographs Division [LC-D4-90156])*

- *July 26:* Confederate cavalryman John Hunt Morgan is captured by Union forces at New Lisbon, Ohio. Morgan and his men have covered 700 miles in one month, sometimes averaging 60 miles per day.
- *August 21:* About 450 guerrilla fighters for the Confederacy descend on Lawrence, Kansas. Led by William Quantrill, the raiders kill about 150 men and boys and lay waste to the town.
- *September 19–20:* Gen. Braxton Bragg leads the Confederates in the Battle of Chickamauga, Georgia. The Confederates gain the advantage, and only Bragg's timidity prevents them from scoring a major success. Union general George Thomas stands firm while other regiments collapse, leading to the nickname "the Rock of Chickamauga." Bragg is unable or unwilling to follow up his success.
- *October 23–November 25:* Grant has been ordered to take charge of the campaign to drive the Confederates away from Chattanooga, Tennessee.

- *October 6:* William Quantrill's Confederate raiders massacre nearly 100 Union troops at Baxter Springs, Kansas.
- *November 19:* Lincoln goes to the Gettysburg battlefield to deliver a special address. Lincoln is preceded that day by Edward Everett, a renowned orator, who goes on for more than two hours. Lincoln then takes the platform. He delivers a four-minute address that contains only 272 words, beginning with, "Four score and seven years ago our fathers brought forth, upon this continent, a new nation, conceived in liberty, and dedicated to the proposition that all men are created equal." Those who heard him that day, and the countless millions who have since read the words, generally agree that the address is one of the finest expressions of a nation's ideals that has ever been articulated.
- *November 24–25:* Battles of Lookout Mountain and Missionary Ridge. With Grant commanding, Generals Sherman, Hooker, and Thomas lead the assault on the strong defensive positions held by General Bragg's Confederates. The Union troops take Lookout Mountain on November 24 and push the Confederates back from Missionary Ridge the next day; Gen. Philip Sheridan is especially aggressive in this action. The Confederate retreat turns into a rout. The only woman to witness the two battles was "Mother" Ann Bickerdyke, who quickly had her hands full with the sick and wounded.
- *November 26:* Confederate cavalryman John Morgan and six of his officers make a spectacular escape from the penitentiary in Columbus, Ohio.

1864

- *January 11:* Missouri senator John Henderson proposes a joint resolution to draft an amendment to abolish slavery in the United States.
- *February 1:* Lincoln orders that 500,000 men be drafted on March 10, to serve for a period of three years.
- *February 17:* The CSS *H. L. Hunley,* a crude submarine that has already cost at least 25 lives during its trials, pulls up close to the USS *Housatonic* off Charleston, South Carolina, and sinks it with what appears to be a torpedo. However, the Confederate submarine also sinks with the loss of at least eight men; five of the *Housatonic's* crew are lost.
- *February 24:* General Bragg is given the responsibility of chief of staff for the Confederacy. Despite his setbacks and missed opportunities in 1863, Bragg retains the trust of Jefferson Davis.

- *March 2:* Now convinced that he has found the right man, Lincoln nominates Ulysses S. Grant to command all Union land forces, with the rank of lieutenant general; on this day the U.S. Senate confirms the appointment. (The three-star rank had not been awarded since it was first given to George Washington.) Henry Halleck, the former commanding general, returns to his former post as army chief of staff.
- *March 8:* Grant has traveled from Tennessee, and Lincoln meets him for the first time at a White House reception. As is usually the case, Grant does not impress many in a social setting; Only on the battle-field does his presence become remarkable. He and Lincoln, though, strike up an immediately positive working relationship.
- *March 9:* Grant leaves Washington, D.C., for his headquarters at Brandy Station, Virginia. Although General Meade is to remain as commander of the Army of the Potomac, it is clear that Grant is going to make the important decisions.
- *April 12:* Fort Pillow, Tennessee, is manned by about 550 Union troops, about half of whom are blacks. Gen. Nathan Bedford Forrest leads a Confederate attack that ends up storming the fort. Union casualties include 231 killed, 100 seriously wounded. The Federals later claim they surrendered when they saw that all was lost but that the Confederates persisted in slaughtering them, especially the black troops; the Confederates insist that all the casualties resulted from a fair battle.
- *May 4–5:* The Army of the Potomac crosses the Rapidan River and advances south into the part of Virginia known as the Wilderness.
- *May 5:* General Sherman leaves Chattanooga, headed east toward Atlanta.
- *May 5–7:* Grant and Lee's armies collide in the Battle of the Wilder-ness. Lee, who has barely half the men available to Grant, puts up an enormous effort, hoping to discourage yet another Union general. Instead, Grant and his troops rest, and then continue forward, even though they have suffered 17,000 men killed, wounded, or missing.
- *May 7–September 2:* In northern Georgia, General Sherman sets off on his campaign to take Atlanta. Week by week he slowly pushes back the Confederate forces, commanded by Gen. Joseph Johnston.
- *May 8–20:* Confederate and Union troops clash in a series of skir-mishes and battles that are collectively known as Spotsylvania Court House. Unlike the Wilderness, the fighting is in the open, and the

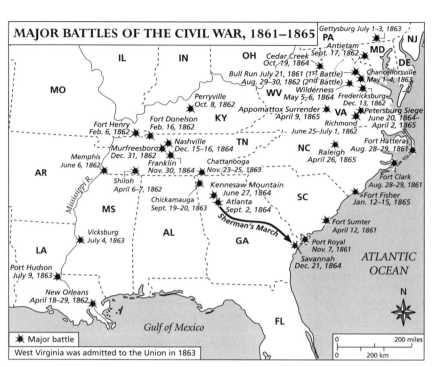

MAJOR BATTLES OF THE CIVIL WAR, 1861–1865

Gettysburg July 1–3, 1863
Antietam Sept. 17, 1862
Cedar Creek Oct. 19, 1864
Bull Run July 21, 1861 (1st Battle)
Aug. 29–30, 1862 (2nd Battle)
Chancellorsville May 1–4, 1863
Wilderness May 5–6, 1864
Fredericksburg Dec. 13, 1862
Perryville Oct. 8, 1862
Appomattox Surrender April 9, 1865
Petersburg Siege June 20, 1864– April 2, 1865
Fort Donelson Feb. 16, 1862
Fort Henry Feb. 6, 1862
Richmond June 25–July 1, 1862
Nashville Dec. 15–16, 1864
Murfreesboro Dec. 31, 1862
Fort Hatteras Aug. 28–29, 1861
Raleigh April 26, 1865
Memphis June 6, 1862
Franklin Nov. 30, 1864
Chattanooga Nov. 23–25, 1863
Fort Clark Aug. 28–29, 1861
Shiloh April 6–7, 1862
Kennesaw Mountain June 27, 1864
Fort Fisher Jan. 12–15, 1865
Chickamauga Sept. 19–20, 1863
Atlanta Sept. 2, 1864
Sherman's March
Fort Sumter April 12, 1861
Vicksburg July 4, 1863
Port Royal Nov. 7, 1861
Savannah Dec. 21, 1864
ATLANTIC OCEAN
Port Hudson July 9, 1863
New Orleans April 18–29, 1862
Gulf of Mexico
N
Major battle
West Virginia was admitted to the Union in 1863
0   200 miles
0   200 km

casualties continue to mount on both sides. Undaunted by the casualties and by criticism, Grant telegraphs Lincoln, "I propose to fight it out on this line if it takes all summer." This one sentence demonstrates a profound difference between Grant and his predecessors, for it implies that he is willing to suffer heavy casualties.

- *May 9–24:* Sheridan leads a daring cavalry raid into Confederate territory. He does not get into Richmond, but at Yellow Tavern, on May 11, he defeats the Confederates under Jeb Stuart, who is mortally wounded.

- *June 3:* Grant launches a head-on assault on the Confederate position at Cold Harbor. In a mistake that is reminiscent of Fredericksburg and Gettysburg, Grant suffers 7,000 men killed, wounded, or missing.

- *June 7–8:* The Republican Party nominates Lincoln again but turns to Tennessee's Andrew Johnson as vice president to retain more moderate voters.

- *June 15–18:* Grant has decided to take Petersburg, a crucial rail junction south of Richmond; he figures that he can then cut Lee and his forces off from supplies of all kinds and isolate Richmond. On these days, Grant directs a series of assaults on the Confederates in Petersburg, but they are beaten back. After the last on August 18, and with casualties totaling some 12,000, he decides that he must resort to a siege.

- *June 19:* The USS *Kearsarge* and CSS *Alabama* fight a two-hour battle off the coast of Cherbourg, France. The *Alabama,* which has sunk, burned, or captured 69 Union vessels in the last two years, goes to the bottom. Its captain, Raphael Semmes, escapes and makes his way to England.

- *June 19–April 3, 1865:* For 10 months, Union forces maintain a siege around Petersburg. Both Lee and Grant take personal charge of their respective forces although neither remains on the scene all of that time. Numerous minor battles and skirmishes are fought in the region of Virginia around Petersburg.

- *June 27:* General Sherman launches a premature attack on Confederate defenses at Kennesaw Mountain in Georgia. The Federals lose 2,500 killed, wounded, or missing, but Sherman will continue with his same aggressive tactics as he moves toward Atlanta.

- *July 11–12:* Confederate cavalry commander Jubal Early reaches Silver Spring, Maryland, within sight of Washington, D.C. Early prepares to attack Washington, but withdraws after he learns that the Federal Sixth Corps has arrived to protect the capital.

- *July 30:* Union soldiers—former coal miners—besieging Petersburg have dug tunnels from their lines to just inside the Confederate defenses. The main shaft is about 510 feet long. The tunnels are filled with some 8,000 pounds of powder, which is exploded about 4:45 A.M. on July 30. The plan was for Union troops to rush forward through the crater, but due to poor execution and delays, the Confederates have time to mount a successful defense. Union casualties amount to some 3,800, and the Confederate losses were less than half that.

- *August 5:* A Union fleet under Admiral Farragut enters Mobile Bay, Alabama. The harbor is protected by forts and submerged mines. One of the Union ships hits a submerged mine and sinks at once. When someone suggests the fleet turn around, Farragut shouts: "Damn the torpedoes—full speed ahead!" The Union ships continue, and enter the harbor where they succeed in destroying all the Confederate ships.

- *August 7–March 2, 1865:* Sheridan conducts what is conceded to be a brilliant and daring campaign in the Shenandoah Valley, defeating

Federal troops, overseen by Gen. William Sherman (in the background), man a captured Confederate fort in Atlanta. Beginning in May 1864, General Sherman had progressively penetrated Georgia, capturing the state's industrial center of Atlanta on September 1. *(National Archives, Still Pictures Branch, NWDNS-165-C-729)*

the Confederates at several engagements, most notably at Winchester (September 19) and Cedar Creek (October 19). But his campaign is also marked by his seizing of every available food source and destruction of many structures and operations such as barns, mills, and railroad lines.

- *September 1:* General Hood evacuates his troops from Atlanta.
- *September 2:* General Sherman's troops occupy Atlanta. Sherman telegraphs Washington, D.C., that "Atlanta is ours and fairly won." The news provides a major boost for the reelection hopes of Lincoln.
- *September 4:* In a surprise attack by Federals, Confederate general John Morgan is shot and killed at Greeneville, Tennessee.
- *September 8:* General McClellan accepts the Democratic Party's nomination for president.
- *October 19:* A small unit of Confederates crosses the Canadian border and raid St. Albans, Vermont. The raiders return to Canada. Newspaper editorials in the North call for an invasion of Canada, but Lincoln and Secretary of State Seward stick to their plan of "one enemy at a time."

- *November 5:* Abraham Lincoln defeats his former general, George B. McClellan, in the presidential election. The popular vote is 2,206,938 for Lincoln and 1,803,787 for McClellan. Andrew Johnson of Tennessee is the vice-president-elect.
- *November 15:* Sherman begins his "March to the Sea." His 60,000 men fan out in a swath that is 60 miles wide. Like Grant and Sheridan, Sherman is committed to the concept of "total war," which means conducting the battle in every conceivable way, including seizing or destroying civilian property if it has any value to the warring armies.
- *November 30:* At Franklin, Tennessee, General Hood makes a frontal attack on Union forces led by Gen. James Schofield. Hood suffers 6,000 casualties, three times the number of the defenders.
- *December 21:* Sherman's men enter and occupy Savannah, Georgia. Sherman telegraphs Lincoln, "I beg to present to you as a Christmas gift the city of Savannah."

Sherman's troops use wheelbarrows to remove ammunition from Fort McAllister after capturing Savannah, Georgia. *(Library of Congress Collection at U.S. Army Military History Institute)*

1865

- *January 12–15:* Union ships commanded by Adm. David Porter conduct a heavy bombardment of Fort Fisher, guarding the port of Wilmington, North Carolina. Union troops under Gen. Alfred Terry then assault and capture the fort.
- *January 31:* The U.S. House of Representatives approves the Thirteenth Amendment—abolishing slavery—by a 119-56-8 vote. On December 18, 1865, two-thirds of the states will have approved the amendment and it will become law.
- *February 1:* General Sherman's army crosses into South Carolina.
- *February 6:* Jefferson Davis appoints Gen. John Breckinridge Confederate secretary of war. Robert E. Lee receives orders to take the duties of general-in-chief of the Armies of the Confederate States.
- *February 17:* Union troops enter Columbia, South Carolina.
- *March 4:* Abraham Lincoln and Andrew Johnson are sworn in as president and vice president. Lincoln's speech is marked by a desire for reconciliation: "with malice toward none; with charity for all." Johnson's acceptance speech is marred by slurred speech and demeanor; he had drunk a good deal in order to conceal his nerves, but the plan backfired.
- *March 13:* Confederate president Jefferson Davis signs a bill that would allow Confederates to arm their slaves for service in the Confederate army.
- *April 1:* Lee leads the remnants of the Army of Northern Virginia, some 35,000 hungry and weary men, out of Richmond and Petersburg. He is immediately pursued by the entire Army of the Potomac, more than 100,000 men.
- *April 4:* Accompanied by his 12-year old son, Tad, and by 10 sailors, Lincoln enters the captured Richmond. The former Confederate capital is reduced to a mere shell of what it had once been.
- *April 6:* At the Battle of Sayler's Creek, the Union forces in pursuit continue to knock away Lee's hopes for escape.
- *April 9:* Lee and Grant meet at the home of Wilmer McLean at Appomattox Court House, Virginia. (McLean had lived at Manassas until 1861, but the First Battle of Bull Run had persuaded him to move somewhere else for peace and quiet.) Lee surrenders the Army of Northern Virginia on the understanding that his men will be able to retain their sidearms and their horses and mules for the spring

plowing. This is the third time that a major Confederate army has surrendered to Grant: the first two occasions were at Fort Donelson in 1862 and Vicksburg in 1863. The surrender ceremony is marked by the solemn demeanor of both men and an earnest desire for reconciliation.

- *April 13:* Lincoln suspends the draft.
- *April 14:* John Wilkes Booth shoots President Lincoln at Ford's Theatre in Washington, D.C. Fellow conspirators seriously wound Secretary of State Seward.
- *April 15:* President Lincoln dies early in the morning. Within the next few weeks, condolences pour in from around the world. Even the British magazine *Punch,* which had vilified Lincoln in cartoons during 1861 and 1862, now laments, "He was our best friend." Andrew Johnson is sworn in as the new president of the United States.
- *April 26:* General Johnston surrenders to General Sherman at Durham Station, North Carolina.
- *April 26:* John Wilkes Booth is shot and killed in Bowling Green, Virginia.
- *April 27:* The steamship *Sultana* explodes on the Mississippi River near Memphis. The ship, whose capacity was 400 people, had about 2,000 people aboard, most of them Union soldiers returning from Confederate prison camps. About 1,700 people die in the disaster, the worst such maritime disaster in U.S. history.
- *May 4:* Lincoln is buried in Springfield, Illinois.
- *May 10:* William Quantrill is surprised and captured near Louisville, Kentucky, by Federal guerrillas who have been assigned to track him down. Wounded during his capture, Quantrill dies in a military prison one month later.
- *May 10:* Jefferson Davis, his wife, and some other Confederate dignitaries are captured near Irwinville, Georgia.
- *May 12–13:* At Palmetto Ranch, Texas, the last significant battle of the war takes place. Although the Confederates drive off the Union troops, they will then have to abandon the struggle.
- *May 23–24:* In Washington, D.C., some 150,000 Union troops parade before President Andrew Johnson and various generals.
- *June 2:* At Galveston, Texas, Confederate general Kirby Smith surrenders the last major Confederate force. This is often regarded as the end of the Civil War.

General Grant, President Johnson, and the cabinet make a "grand review" of the Union army as it parades through Washington, D.C. *(National Archives, Still Pictures Branch, NWDNS-111-B-54)*

- *June 23:* Cherokee chief Stand Watie and his last group of Confederate followers surrender in the Oklahoma Territory.
- *November:* The Confederate raider *Shenandoah* surrenders to British authorities at Liverpool, England. It had captured or destroyed 36 vessels in the past year.

Results

The casualty figures speak for themselves: about 620,000 men killed, wounded, or missing on the two sides combined. (This does not include civilian deaths, largely in the South.) The military casualties exceed the combined total of all American military casualties in every other war since the Civil War, including World War II. The cost in dollars is incalculable, especially if such items as veterans' pensions are factored in; property losses, mainly in the South, are vast; as a rough estimate, the total cost for both sides is probably around $500 billion (in 2002 dollars). But set against such calculations is the fact that some 4,000,000 African Americans are freed, and the idea of the Union as permanent and indivisible has won a complete victory over the idea of the Union as a compact of sovereign states, each of which may withdraw when it chooses.

5

THE PLAINS
INDIAN WARS

By the mid-19th century, Indian groups on the western plains had developed a variety of lifestyles adapted to the immediate environment. Some tribes depended primarily on hunting buffalo, while others engaged in agriculture. There was some warring among themselves, but basically the tribes maintained a state of equilibrium. The Native peoples did not, however, anticipate the flood of non-Native Americans who pressed in on their lands, increasingly after about the year 1850.

1851

- *July–August:* Dakota Sioux leaders sign the Treaty of 1851. The Dakota Sioux cede all their remaining land in Minnesota with the exception of a reservation that runs on both sides of the Minnesota River.
- *September:* Roughly 10,000 Indians meet with U.S. negotiators at Horse Creek, 34 miles east of Fort Laramie, in southeast Wyoming. Thomas "Broken Hand" Fitzpatrick, a former fur trader, arranges the conference. Among other matters, the treaty assigns various tribes to specific lands; commits the United States to pay an annual fee that the Indians must come to Fort Laramie to collect; and states that non-Indians will try and punish non-Indians who commit crimes or breaks rules, while Indians will do the same with anyone in their tribe who commits a crime or breaks a rule.

1854

- *April:* Dakota chief Little Crow travels to Washington, D.C. He tries, but fails, to have the size of the Dakota reservation increased.
- *August 18:* In Wyoming, a cow belonging to a Mormon wagon train is killed. Suspicion falls upon local Sioux (Dakota, Lakota, Nakota) Indians.
- *August 19:* U.S. lieutenant John Grattan leaves Fort Laramie to accost the Sioux over the incident with the Mormons. The Indians detest the recent West Point graduate, who is known for his bellicose behavior. The Sioux offer money reparation, as provided for under the Treaty of 1851. Someone fires a first shot, and all but one of 27 U.S. soldiers are killed. The one survivor brings the news to Fort Laramie.

1855

- *Summer:* Col. William Harney leads a punitive expedition against the Sioux.
- *September 3:* Harney destroys Little Thunder's village on the Blue-water River.

1858

- Gold is discovered at Pikes Peak, Colorado. Between 1858 and 1862, 80,000 emigrants will arrive in the Rocky Mountain region. Meanwhile, settlers from east of the Mississippi and even Europe continue to make their way west along the Oregon Trail and other routes, and increasing numbers of them are settling in the Great Plains.

1861

- *February 4:* A U.S. Army unit led by Lt. George Bascom arrives at Apache Pass in southeastern Arizona. They arrest Cochise, an Apache war chief, who has been falsely accused of kidnapping a white boy, and three relatives. Cochise escapes captivity and then seizes three white men, whom he kills after the army refuses to make a hostage exchange. The army then kills Cochise's three relatives, and the Cochise War begins.
- *April 12:* The Civil War begins. While the Plains Indians have little involvement with the war, they soon notice that the bluecoats (U.S. soldiers) are fewer in number for the next four years.

- *Summer:* Apache led by Cochise and his father-in-law, war leader Mangas Coloradas, attack white travelers and settlers and seal off Apache Pass in southeastern Arizona, thus cutting off a main route to California.

1862

- John Bozeman, a gold prospector, finds a shortcut across southern Montana when passing west from northeastern Wyoming to the now booming mining camps of Virginia City and Helena. The U.S. Army is preoccupied with the war but will soon decide to build a series of forts along the Bozeman Trail even though the land has been assigned to the Sioux.
- *May 20:* President Abraham Lincoln signs the Homestead Act, which opens the federal lands in the West to non-Indian pioneer settlers.
- *July 1:* Lincoln signs the Transcontinental Railroad Bill.
- *Summer:* The Dakota in Minnesota are facing starvation so Chief Little Crow asks Indian Agent Thomas Galbraith to provide food for his people. When Galbraith says he cannot help, Little Crow replies: "When men are hungry they help themselves."
- *July 15:* In Apache Pass, pro-Union troops led by Gen. James Carleton are ambushed by Apache. The next day the troops retaliate with howitzers, and the Indians suffer heavy casualties. Mangas Coloradas is wounded, and Cochise takes him down into Mexico for treatment.
- *August 4:* Santee Dakota Sioux break into a warehouse on their Minnesota reservation. The settlers open fire and the Indians retreat.
- *August 18–23:* The Great Sioux Uprising begins in Minnesota when in the course of these six days some 400 white Americans die in an unprecedented series of attacks by the Santee Dakota. The principal Santee Dakota leader is Little Crow.
- *August 23:* Santee Dakota warriors attack New Ulm on the Minnesota River. The town is nearly destroyed, but the inhabitants hold out.
- *August 28:* Col. Henry Hastings Sibley has been commissioned to raise a force to put down the Santee Dakota. With the arrival of the first of these men at Fort Ridgely, near the Santee Da-

kota reservation, Little Crow withdraws to the north but he takes some 200 whites with him, about half of whom are women and children.

- *September 23:* Colonel Sibley defeats the Santee Dakota in a battle at Wood Lake, at the junction of the Yellow Medicine and Minnesota Rivers. Although the Santee Dakota casualties were relatively light— about 30 killed—this defeat effectively ended the Santee Dakota resistance.
- *September 26:* Sibley takes numerous Santee Dakota captives, and some 270 white captives are freed. Little Crow flees into Canada.
- *November:* After the military trials of some 400 Dakota, 303 Santee Dakota are sentenced to be hanged. Many people question this, but the most effective protest seems to be that of Episcopal bishop Henry Whipple, who appeals to President Lincoln to reconsider the fate of the Santee Dakota captives.
- *December 26:* President Lincoln has reviewed the case of all 303 Santee Dakota and determines that only those convicted of murder or rape should be executed. On this day, 38 Santee Dakota are hanged in a mass execution at Mankato, Minnesota. It is the largest mass execution in U.S. history.

1863

- *January 17:* Mangas Coloradas is seized while under a flag of truce.
- *January 19:* American soldiers execute Mangas Coloradas. The soldiers scalp Mangas Coloradas and throw his body into a ditch; their commander informs Washington that the leader had been killed while trying to escape. This action is long remembered by the Apache, who continue to harass white settlers and federal troops throughout the duration of the Civil War.
- *May:* Little Crow, leader of a band of Mdewakanton Dakota, requests help from the British in Canada. Governor Alexander Dallas in Winnipeg refuses assistance.
- *June:* George Armstrong Custer is made brigadier general of volunteers in the Union army. He is the youngest general on either side of the fighting.
- *June:* Little Crow returns to Minnesota.
- *July 3:* Little Crow is ambushed and killed by Minnesota farmers.

CHRONOLOGY OF WARS

1864

- *April 11:* A Colorado rancher reports some of his livestock have been rustled by Cheyenne Indians. A U.S. detachment from Fort Sanborn is dispatched and fights the first clash of the Cheyenne-Arapaho War.
- *June:* Cheyenne and Arapaho warriors continue to attack settlers in the central region of Colorado. Colorado governor John Evans appeals to Washington, D.C., for troops. Washington says that the Colorado troops are needed in the ongoing Civil War.
- *September 28:* Governor Evans and Col. John Chivington, commander of a newly formed Colorado regiment, meet with many Cheyenne and Arapaho at Camp Weld, outside Denver. The Indians agree to cease hostilities. By November, many of the Indians will be camp-

ENGAGEMENTS WITH INDIANS, 19TH CENTURY

CANADA

Puget Sound Fights (1856)
Four Lakes (1858)
Rains Fight (1855)
Steptoe Defeat (1858)
Marias (1870)
Whitman Agency (1847)
Clearwater (1877)
Little Bighorn (1876)
Lame Deer (1877)
Killdeer Mtn. (1864)
Powder River (1875)
Dead Buffalo Lake (1863)
Birch Creek (1878)
Grande Ronde Valley (1878)
Whitebird (1877)
Hayfield (1867)
Stoney Lake (1863)
Big Mound (1863)
Big Meadows (1856)
Big Hole (1878)
Rosebud (1876)
Slim Buttes (1876)
Whitestone Hill (1863)
Steen Mtn. (1878)
Wagon Box (1867)
Wolf Mountain (1877)
Wood Lake (1862)
Birch Coulee (1862)
Ft. Ridgely (1862)
Lost River (1872)
Lava Beds (1873)
Dry Lake (1873)
Dull Knife (1876)
Platte Bridge (1865)
Fetterman Fight (1866)
New Ulm (1862)
Bear Creek (1863)
Grattan Affair (1854)
War Bonnet Creek (1876)
Wounded Knee (1890)
Pyramid Lake (1860)
Milk Creek (1879)
Summit Springs (1879)
Blue Water (1855)
Julesburg (1865)
Meeker Agency (1879)
Massacre Canyon (1873)
Beecher Island (1868)
Beaver Creek (1868)
Sand Creek (1864)
Crooked Creek (1859)
Canyon de Chelly (1864)
Big Dry Wash (1862)
Taos (1847)
Adobe Walls (1864, 1874)
Antelope Hills (1858)
Salt River Canyon (1872)
Cibecue Creek (1881)
McClellan Creek (1872)
Palo Duro Canyon (1874)
Washita (1868)
Skull Cave (1872)
Camp Grant (1871)
Apache Pass (1862)
Rush Springs (1858)
Soldier Spring (1868)
Skeleton Canyon (1886)
Canyon de los Embudos (1886)
Dove Creek (1865)
Tres Castillos (1880)

PACIFIC OCEAN

N

MEXICO

Gulf of Mexico

Lake Superior

0   400 miles
0   400 km

✹ Major battle

Modern state boundaries provided for reference.

ing 40 miles away, at Sand Creek. Their chief Black Kettle wants to avoid hostilities.

- *November 28–29:* Leading his force of some 1,000 men, Colonel Chivington makes a night march and on the morning of November 29, leads his cavalry in an unabashed slaughter of Cheyenne men, women, and children peacefully camping at Sand Creek. It is estimated that some 163 Indians are killed, most of them women and children. Black Kettle escapes.

1865

- *January–February:* Now enraged over the slaughter at Sand Creek, Cheyenne, Arapaho, and Sioux warriors hit white settlements throughout the South Platte Valley in Colorado.
- *April–June:* The Civil War ends and Confederate units from Virginia to North Carolina and as far west as Texas surrender. The war's end will allow the federal government to send far more troops to western areas to battle Indians.
- *July 26:* More than 1,000 warriors attack the U.S. military station at Upper Platte Bridge in Colorado.
- *Summer:* Gen. Patrick Connor pursues the Sioux and Arapaho into the Teton Mountain area. His campaign is a failure.

1866

- *Summer:* Col. Henry Carrington leads some 700 soldiers, many with family members accompanying them, from Nebraska, eventually picking up the Bozeman Trail to the Powder River, east of the Bighorn Mountains. There, in northern Wyoming, he proceeds to build Fort Phil Kearny (named after a Civil War hero). Oglala Lakota Sioux led by Red Cloud soon begin to attack, and the fort will effectively be under siege for the next two years.
- *December 21:* Capt. William Fetterman has been assigned to help in the defense of Fort Phil Kearny. Against the advice of more knowledgeable men, Fetterman leads his force of 80 men away from the fort and, falling for a trap, he is ambushed by Sioux and Cheyenne warriors. Fetterman and his entire detachment are killed. White Americans call it the Fetterman Massacre; the Indians call it the Battle of the Hundred Slain. Gen. William Sherman, commander of all the western forces, calls for all-out war against the Indians along the Bozeman Trail.

Indians surround Captain Fetterman's troops near Fort Phil Kearny.
(Library of Congress, Prints & Photographs Division [LC-USZ62-130184])

1867

- *August 2:* Capt. James Powell and his men successfully defend their wagons at the Wagon Box Fight. The Indians, who are driven off, call it the Medicine Fight, believing that the soldiers must have had good medicine to survive that day.
- *Summer:* Gen. Winfield Scott Hancock tries but fails to subdue the Sioux and Cheyenne in Kansas, Colorado, and Nebraska.
- *October 21–28:* Chiefs of the Kiowa, Comanche, Cheyenne, and Arapaho tribes sign a treaty at Medicine Lodge Creek, Kansas; they agree to move into large reservations in the Indian Territory (present-day Oklahoma). Red Cloud, however, refuses to agree to such a treaty.

1868

- *April:* General Sherman leads a "peace commission" that sits down with Indian leaders at Fort Laramie in Wyoming. He agrees to abandon three forts along the Bozeman Trail—Reno, C. F. Smith, and

Philip Kearny—and in return, some of the Indian chiefs sign a treaty restoring their claim on the territory that includes the Dakotas west of the Missouri River and the Black Hills.

- *September 17–24:* Sioux and Cheyenne warriors kill a number of soldiers and scouts on a small island in the Arikaree River in northeastern Colorado. The whites call it the Battle of Beecher's Island after a U.S. officer killed there, but the Indians call it after Chief Roman Nose who was also killed there.
- *November 7:* Red Cloud finally signs the Treaty of Fort Laramie. This is a moment he has long waited for, and the chief delivers a stinging oration against U.S. policy after he signs.
- *November 27:* Col. George Custer's Seventh Cavalry carries out an early morning surprise attack and destroys most of the band of Black Kettle's Cheyenne sleeping along the Washita River in western Oklahoma. Black Kettle, who had escaped the Sand Creek Massacre, was killed along with his wife.

Colonel Custer's troops attack a Cheyenne encampment along the Washita River. *(Library of Congress, Prints & Photographs Division [LC-USZ62-130899])*

1869

- *February:* President-elect Ulysses S. Grant tells a newspaper reporter that "All Indians disposed to peace will find the new policy a peace policy."
- *March 18:* In the Texas Panhandle, Custer has been negotiating with some Cheyenne for two days to get them to release two white women. He seizes four chiefs and threatens to kill them, so the Indians agree to release the women and return to their reservation. Only Chief Tall Bull and his band refuses the terms.
- *May 10:* Officials of the Union Pacific and Overland Pacific Railroad companies celebrate the driving of the "Golden Spike," joining the two lines to complete the first transcontinental railroad.
- *July 11:* U.S. Cavalry surprise Tall Bull and his band at Summit Springs, in northeastern Colorado, and kill him and almost all of his 200 Cheyenne.

1871

- *April 30:* Angered by the Apache raids, a group of vigilantes from around Tucson, Arizona, carry out a surprise attack on an Apache encampment near the San Pedro River, massacre some 90–150 people and sell 27 Apache children into slavery. Although put on trial, the organizers are not found guilty.
- *September:* Cochise meets with U.S. Army officers to work out a truce, but when informed that he would have to move his people to a reservation in south-central New Mexico, he goes back into the mountains of southeastern Arizona with his followers.

1872

- *October:* Cochise meets General Howard in the Dragoon Mountains. The two confer for more than two weeks. Cochise insists on many conditions and wins most of them. He is given control of Apache Pass, and a reservation is created in his ancestral country.
- *November 15:* Under Gen. George Crook, the U.S. Army launches an offensive against the Apache still raiding in central Arizona.

1873

- *January:* President Grant sends a peace commission to deal with the Indians in Utah.

- *March:* Most of the Apache in Arizona have been put down, and they are settling into reservations. Cochise himself will soon follow.

1874

- *March:* A large group of Comanche, Kiowa, Cheyenne, and Arapaho hold a three-day Sun Dance in the Texas Panhandle. Isatai, a Cheyenne medicine man, becomes prominent. He promises the warriors they will be protected from the white men's bullets by his medicine.
- *June 27:* Indian warriors led by Quanah Parker (son of a Comanche chief and a white woman) attack Adobe Walls, a trading post, in northeastern Texas. The post holds out until reinforcements arrive; then they abandon the post. The Indians suffer so many casualties that Isatai is quickly repudiated; his medicine has not protected the warriors from harm.
- *July 27:* Col. George A. Custer's men confirm the presence of gold in the Black Hills, which are in Sioux country according to the 1868 Fort Laramie Treaty. Custer magnifies the discovery in his report, making it seem as if gold is there for the picking. The *Bismarck Tribune* echoes Custer and goes even further: "Humanitarians may weep for poor [Indian], and tell the wrongs he has suffered, but he is passing away. Their prayers, their entreaties can not change the law of nature."
- *August 30:* Col. Nelson Miles, engages 200 Cheyenne at Mulberry Creek, in northwestern Texas. When the Cheyenne begin to retreat, they are reinforced by Comanche and Kiowa and eventually Miles is forced to stop his pursuit.
- *September:* At Palo Duran canyon in the Texas Panhandle, Col. Ranald Mackenzie leads his troop of some 475 men against Comanche Indians; although casualties on both sides are light, the Indians are forced to abandon some 1,500 ponies. More and more Indians in the Southwest are now finding themselves overwhelmed by the superior numbers and arms of U.S. Army forces in the region.

1875

- During this year, the U.S. government begins to force the Apache bands into the large new San Carlos Reservation, located in the arid Gila River Valley in southeastern Arizona. Among those who continue to resist is a band led by a war chief Goyathlay—known to the whites as Geron-imo. He will lead hundreds of Apache in ongoing attacks on whites.

Gold prospectors start to find their way into the Black Hills.

- *January–May:* Subdued by the cold winter and lack of food, increasing numbers of Comanche and Cheyenne are turning themselves in to reservations.
- *April 23:* U.S. Cavalry kill some 30 Cheyenne at Sappa Creek in northwest Kansas.

1876

- *January 31:* A deadline passes: The U.S. government had selected this day as the deadline for the Sioux to return to their reservations.
- *Spring:* Gen. Philip Sheridan draws up a three-pronged campaign to return the Sioux to their reservation. Gen. George Crook is to advance north from Wyoming; Col. John Gibbon is to move east from Fort Ellis in western Montana; and Gen. Alfred Terry to move west from Dakota. Colonel Custer is to command the Seventh Cavalry under Terry.
- *May:* The Sioux hold a major Sun Dance in the Black Hills. Chief Sitting Bull has a vision in which he sees enemy soldiers falling in great numbers.
- *May 17:* General Terry and Colonel Custer leave Fort Lincoln in the Dakota Territory.
- *June 17:* Battle of Rosebud Creek, about 20 miles north of the Wyoming-Montana border. Crazy Horse leads about 1,500 warriors in an attack on 1,300 U.S. troops led by General Crook. The battle is a standoff, but Crazy Horse has stopped the U.S. penetration of the area.
- *June 25:* The Battle of the Little Bighorn, in southern Montana. Sioux warriors led by Crazy Horse and Sitting Bull attack Custer's small detachment. All 275 members of Custer's command perish in one day. Accounts of the battle vary widely. Some Indians claim Custer and his men were quickly subdued; other accounts testify that it was a long and grueling battle.
- *July–August:* News of "Custer's last stand" arrives just as the United States celebrates its centennial with ceremonies in Philadelphia and throughout the land. The news ignites a firestorm in U.S. public opinion. About 4,000 men are sent to reinforce Generals Terry and Crook.
- *August–September:* Generals Terry and Crook cut a wide swath

A horse-drawn stretcher carries a wounded man from the Battle of Slim Buttes, Dakota, 1876. *(National Archives, Still Pictures Branch, NWDNS-111-SC-85704)*

through Montana, searching for the Indians. Most of the Indians have dispersed into small bands and cannot be found.

- *September 9:* Some 2,000 U.S. troops pursue Indians north of the Black Hills in South Dakota when they come upon a large camp of Sioux at Slim Buttes. In the fierce fight that ensues, the sheer numbers of U.S. soldiers eventually prevail and the Sioux flee, leaving behind a large amount of their food and possessions. Although both sides' casualties are relatively light, some Sioux refer to this battle as "The Fight Where We Lost the Black Hills."
- *October:* Gen. Nelson Miles wins a sharp skirmish with Sioux, including Sitting Bull, at Cedar Creek.
- *November 25:* Cavalry commander Ranald Mackenzie surprises and defeats Dull Knife's band in the Bighorn Mountains.

1877

- *January:* General Miles defeats Sioux warriors, led by Crazy Horse, at the Battle of Wolf Mountains.

CHRONOLOGY OF WARS

- *January 9:* U.S. troops led by Lt. J. Rucker defeat Geronimo's Apache band in southwestern New Mexico.
- *April:* Sitting Bull crosses the border to Canada and safety.
- *May:* A council is held at Lapwai, Washington. The Nez Perce agree to assemble their animals and head to the new reservation designated for them.
- *May:* General Miles defeats Lame Deer's Sioux band at the Battle of Muddy Creek.
- *May 6:* Chief Crazy Horse gives himself up at Fort Robinson, Nebraska.
- *June 17:* The Nez Perce War begins when Nez Perce warriors defeat a detachment of U.S. troops at the Battle of White Bird Canyon, near the Salmon River.
- *July 11–12:* Nez Perce warriors defeat a large U.S. force on the Clearwater River.
- *July 15:* The Nez Perce hold a strategic council. They resolve to cross the Bitterroot Mountains into western Montana, and then head northward to safety in Canada.

Crazy Horse on his way to surrender to General Crook on May 6, 1877.
(Library of Congress, Prints & Photographs Division [LC-USZ62-122957])

- *September 5:* Crazy Horse is killed by Little Big Man, an Indian working for the U.S. Army. It remains controversial whether Crazy Horse was killed intentionally.
- *September 13:* The Nez Perce hold back elements of the Seventh Cavalry at the Battle of Canyon Creek.
- *September 30:* General Miles catches up with Chief Joseph's band in the Bear Paw Mountains, just 40 miles short of the Canadian border. Miles surrounds the Nez Perce.
- *October 1–4:* A siege of the Nez Perce takes place.
- *October 5:* Chief Joseph and 400 Nez Perce surrender. Joseph addresses his surrender speech to Gen. Oliver Howard. Chief Joseph concludes: "Hear me my chiefs. I am tired. My heart is sick and sad. From where the sun now stands I will fight no more forever." Joseph soon becomes one of the best-known and admired Indian chiefs. In fact, Joseph was the principal chief in civil matters; his brother Ollikut was the war chief and conducted most of the military action.

1878

- *April 4:* Geronimo escapes from the San Carlos Reservation in Arizona and will continue to attack whites until he surrenders and returns to the San Carlos Reservation.

1879

- *January 9:* Dull Knife and more than 100 Cheyenne escape from Fort Robinson. All but six are shot or captured within the next day.
- *September 4–October 15, 1880:* Apache warriors led by Chief Victorio attack a camp of the U.S. Ninth Cavalry; this instigates a year-long pursuit that ends with Victorio's death in battle.

1880

- *February 12:* President Rutherford B. Hayes issues a warning to the settlers, ranchers, and various other trespassers who have been stealing the land in Indian Territory. This warning goes virtually unheeded.

1881

- Helen Hunt Jackson publishes *A Century of Dishonor,* describing the United States's mistreatment of Indians. The book, published in blood-red covers, is delivered to every major policy maker in Washington, D.C.

- *July 19:* Sitting Bull has come back from Canada and with 186 of his band surrenders at Fort Buford, Dakota Territory.
- *August:* Frederic Remington goes west for the first time. He visits Wyoming and Montana.
- *September:* Geronimo leads a band of Apache south across the Rio Grande and begins to attack Mexicans. The Mexican army counterattacks and kills many of the Apache women and children.

1882

- *February 25: Harper's Weekly* publishes Frederic Remington's sketch of a cowboy in Wyoming. It is his first publication, and the beginning of an illustrious career that helps to define Americans' view of the West.
- *April 19:* Geronimo attacks the San Carlos Reservation and persuades some 5,600 Apache to flee with him into the Sierra Madre in northern Mexico.

1883

- *May:* General Crook crosses into Mexico and, after attacking the Apache camp and taking women and children hostage, forces Geronimo to meet with him. Crook persuades the Indian leader to return to San Carlos Reservation.

1884

- *January:* Geronimo surrenders and is taken to the San Carlos Reservation.

1885

- *May 17:* Geronimo and a handful of followers flee the San Carlos Reservation and go back into the Sierra Madre where he remains at large for the next 16 months.
- *December 1885–January 10, 1886:* Gen. Crook leads another expedition into Mexico and catches up with Geronimo. In the ensuing firefight, Geronimo escapes.

Geronimo (first row, third from right) was among other Apache prisoners being taken to Florida in September 1886. *(National Archives, Still Pictures Division, NWDNS-111-SC-82320)*

1886

- *March 25–28:* General Crook and Geronimo meet at Canyon de los Embudos in northern Mexico. Geronimo and other Apache chiefs agree to Crook's terms. They are to return to the San Carlos Reservation, but when they get to the border, they fear they will be murdered, and on March 28 Geronimo and a small band flee back into the Sierra Madre.
- *April 2:* Impatient with his handling of Geronimo, the U.S. Army replaces General Crook with General Nelson Miles.
- *August:* U.S. lieutenant Charles Gatewood finds Geronimo and persuades him to surrender to General Miles.
- *September 4:* Geronimo surrenders to General Miles at Skeleton Canyon in southeastern Arizona. This effectively ends the Apache Wars. Geronimo will be imprisoned first in Florida then in Oklahoma; freed in 1894, he remained at Fort Sill, Oklahoma, where he died in 1909.

- Sitting Bull joins the Wild West Show of Buffalo Bill (William Frederick) Cody.

1887

- Congress passes the Dawes General Allotment (Severalty) Act. It is designed to break up the remnants of tribal life and encourage the Indians to become individual farmers.

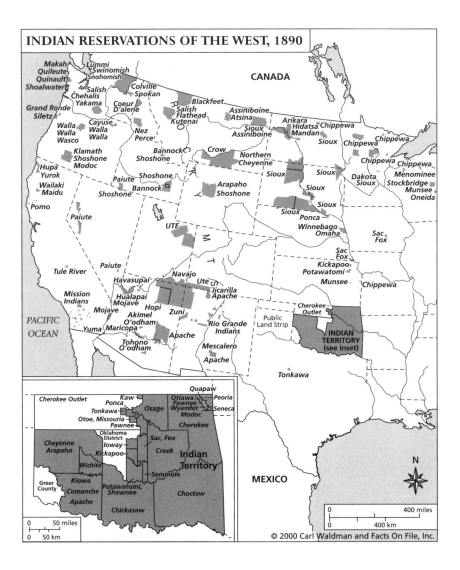

INDIAN RESERVATIONS OF THE WEST, 1890

1888

- *March:* Following a series of earth tremors, the Northern Paiute (Numu) Indian Wovoka (known to whites as Jack Wilson) experiences the first of the visions that will lead to the Ghost Dance Religion.

1889

- *January 1:* Wovoka has a series of visions during a solar eclipse. He sees the buffalo and all Indians who ever lived returning to live again on the Great Plains.

1890

- *March 21:* General Crook dies in Chicago, on the eve of a major news campaign intended to win better treatment for Apache captives.
- *November–December:* Sioux believers in Wovoka's visions hold major Ghost Dances at the Pine Ridge Reservation (southern South Dakota) and the Standing Rock Reservation (northern South Dakota).
- *December 15:* Sitting Bull is killed by Hunkpapa police who are sent to confine him during the Ghost Dances. Some of his followers flee and join Chief Big Foot's band of Miniconjou Lakota Sioux on the Cheyenne River.
- *December 28:* U.S. Cavalry discover Big Foot and some 340 Sioux in the Pine Ridge Reservation. After negotiation, the Indians agree to go peacefully to Wounded Knee Creek, on the reservation in southwest South Dakota.
- *December 28–29:* During the night, the U.S. Seventh Cavalry, Custer's former unit, has converged on the encampment of Sioux at Wounded Knee Creek. In the morning, the troops begin to move through the camp, demanding that the Indians hand over all their firearms. At some point, shots ring out—no one will ever agree as to who fired first. But the Americans have all the firepower, including four rapid-fire Hotchkiss guns on a hill overlooking the camp, and they proceed to massacre as many of the men, women, and children as they can. Estimates of the dead—including Big Foot—range from some 150 to 300.

1891

- *January 14–16:* The last of the Sioux who were off the reservations surrender in small groups.
- The Bureau of the U.S. Census declares that the frontier has closed.

1893

- *July 12:* Historian Frederick Jackson Turner reads a paper, "The Significance of the Frontier in American History," to the American Historical Association, meeting at the World's Fair in Chicago. His thesis is that it has been the frontier that has made America exceptional.
- *September 16:* The largest of the great rushes into Oklahoma Territory occurs, as 50,000 homesteaders make a mad dash to secure land that up to now has been assigned to Native Americans.

Results

It is essentially impossible to assign hard numbers to the casualties on both sides, especially since civilian casualties probably far outnumbered those of the military: A rough estimate would be 5,000 non-Indians and at least twice that many Native Americans. It is also impossible to put a dollar price tag on these wars. But the real point is that the losses (for the Indians) and the gains (for non-Indian citizens of the United States) are incalculable in the most literal sense of that word. The Plains Indians not only lost most of their land and resources, they lost their way of life. The newcomers gained all that and more.

6

THE SPANISH-
AMERICAN WAR

Spaniards dominated Cuba almost from the landing of Columbus in 1492, and centuries of misrule wiped out the native peoples while employing thousands of slaves of African descent. During the Ten Years' War on Cuba (1878–88), some whites joined blacks and people of mixed origins but failed in their struggle to gain independence. They failed but at least succeeded in abolishing slavery.

1895–1897

- José Martí, the leader of increasingly restless Cuban revolutionaries, calls for a war for independence. He is killed by a Spanish cavalry patrol in May 1895, but the struggle continues. Spain's Gen. Valeriano Weyler y Nicolau enforces a harsh policy of relocating thousands of Cubans into what are effectively concentration camps. U.S. newspapers such as William Randolph Hearst's *New York Journal* and Joseph Pulitzer's *World* stir up support for the Cuban rebels by sending well-known journalists and illustrators to Cuba to report on Spanish activities.

1898

- *January 12:* Reacting to the new prime minister of Spain's offer to the rebels to give Cuba home rule, mobs of Spanish-born Cubans riot in Havana.

- *January 25:* The battleship USS *Maine* arrives in Havana harbor in response to the U.S. consul's fears for the safety of Americans in Cuba.
- *February 15:* While at anchor in the harbor of Havana, the USS *Maine* is rocked by two explosions. Within a few minutes, the ship begins to sink to the bottom. Some 266 U.S. sailors are lost in the explosion and the sinking. Among others who proceed to help the survivors is Clara Barton, there in Havana to direct an American Red Cross aid program for the rebels.
- *February 16–20:* U.S. newspapers blare the news across the land with such slogans as "Remember the *Maine!*" But the government's initial response is restrained. "I don't propose to be swept off my feet by the catastrophe," says President McKinley. Many Americans, however, have become supportive of the Cubans' struggle for independence, and they are quick to blame the Spanish.
- *February 21:* A. U.S. naval court of inquiry meets on a tugboat in Havana harbor and concludes that a mine caused the disaster but does not say who is responsible. During the ensuing decades, numerous claims and theories are advanced to establish the true cause of the explosion. In 1978, a U.S. naval investigation concludes that it was a fire that ignited the ship's ammunition stores.
- *March:* President McKinley find himself under increasing pressure from many in Congress and the press to challenge Spain's actions in Cuba. At first he calls for a cease-fire between the Spanish and Cuban forces, but he soon escalates that to a call for full independence for Cuba.
- *April 11:* Before the Spanish agree to the cease-fire, McKinley asks Congress to consider what the United States should do next.
- *April 19:* Congress passes joint resolutions recognizing Cuban independence, demanding that the Spanish withdraw from Cuba, and authorizing the president to use U.S military force to stop the war in Cuba.
- *April 20:* McKinley signs the resolutions.
- *April 21:* The United States and Spain break off diplomatic relations. The U.S. president orders a naval blockade of Cuba's ports.
- *April 22:* The U.S. Navy's North Atlantic Squadron arrives off Havana.
- *April 24:* The U.S. Navy's Asiatic Squadron, commanded by Commodore George Dewey, has been anchored in Hong Kong for several weeks, mainly due to the aggressive young assistant secretary of the

navy, Theodore Roosevelt. On this day, the navy orders Dewey to "commence operations at once, particularly against the Spanish fleet." This can mean only one thing: head for the Philippines, another Spanish colony.

- *April 25:* Congress approves a formal declaration of war, retroactive to April 21.
- *April 27:* The Asiatic Squadron—seven ships, led by Dewey's flagship, the armored cruiser USS *Olympia*—sails unchallenged into Manila Bay in the Philippines.
- *May:* Within days after the declaration of war, 1 million young Americans volunteer for service. Theodore Roosevelt resigns from his post as assistant secretary of the navy and proceeds to raise a volunteer cavalry regiment, soon known as the "Rough Riders." Volunteers proceed to army training camps in several southern states, and by early May, some of the first units, along with regular army troops, are gathering in Tampa, Florida, which is to be the staging point for the

From the *Olympia*, Adm. George Dewey led U.S. forces in the battle of Manila, 1898. *(Library of Congress, Prints and Photographs Division, [LC-D428-728])*

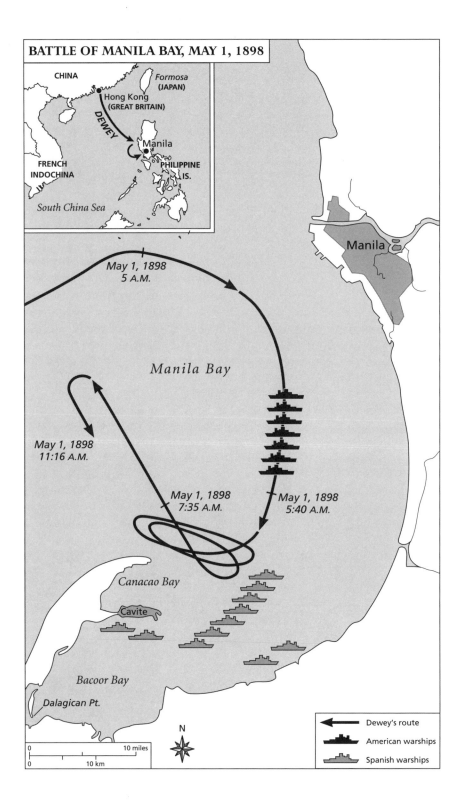

BATTLE OF MANILA BAY, MAY 1, 1898

CHINA

Formosa
(JAPAN)

Hong Kong
(GREAT BRITAIN)

DEWEY

Manila

FRENCH
INDOCHINA

PHILIPPINE
IS.

South China Sea

May 1, 1898
5 A.M.

Manila

Manila Bay

May 1, 1898
11:16 A.M.

May 1, 1898
7:35 A.M.

May 1, 1898
5:40 A.M.

Canacao Bay

Cavite

Bacoor Bay

Dalagican Pt.

N

0   10 miles

0   10 km

Dewey's route

American warships

Spanish warships

invasion of Cuba. Tampa will soon be overwhelmed by the numbers of men and quantities of matériel, and the chaotic logistics will plague the army's operations until the last surviving volunteer is discharged some 16 months later.

- *May 1:* Early in the morning, Dewey discovers that the Spanish fleet is sitting five miles south of the Manila waterfront. The U.S. squadron sails directly at the Spanish fleet, which consists of 10 old and out-classed vessels. By 7:30 A.M. the two largest Spanish ships are out of the action—one of them, the cruiser *Reina Cristina,* having been scuttled by its captain. After taking a break for breakfast, Dewey's ships proceed to sink, wreck, or capture the remaining Spanish ships, and by 12:30 P.M. the Spanish commander surrenders. The Spanish have lost more than 400 men, while only six Americans are wounded. When word of this overwhelming victory reaches the United States, Dewey becomes a national hero.

- *June:* Dewey remains in the Manila harbor with his squadron, in part to keep the German naval forces from trying to take advantage of Spain's weak situation in the Philippines, in part to provide some support to the Filipinos' insurrection against the Spanish being led by Emilio Aguinaldo. By the end of the month, a contingent of U.S. Army troops arrives in the Philippines.

- *June 14:* There has been an ongoing disagreement between the commands of the two services over when to move against the Spanish in Cuba and Puerto Rico: The navy has wanted to attack as soon as possible, the army wants to wait until autumn. The War Department supports the navy, and on this day the great expeditionary force sets sail from Tampa. It is the largest to date to leave the United States for a foreign land: 16,000 troops, 2,500 horses and mules, and large numbers of armaments.

- *June 20:* The first U.S. troops—among them Roosevelt and his Rough Riders—go ashore some 15 miles east of Santiago, on Cuba's southeastern coast. They are unopposed, and the only casualties are two men who drown.

- *June 22:* The U.S. troops advance from their landing beaches toward Santiago.

- *June 24:* In their first encounter with Spanish troops, the Americans suffer 16 dead and 52 wounded but force the Spanish forces to retreat.

- *June 25–30:* The U.S. troops advance toward Santiago only to find that the Spanish have heavily fortified the San Juan Hills that protect

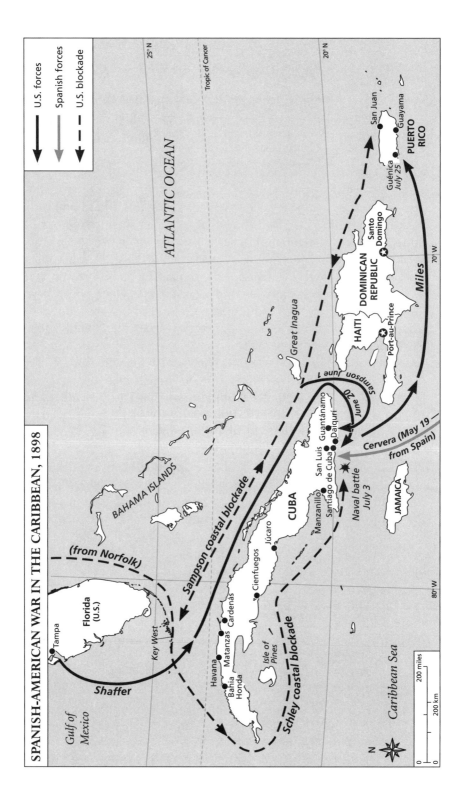

SPANISH-AMERICAN WAR IN THE CARIBBEAN, 1898

Legend:
U.S. forces
Spanish forces
U.S. blockade

ATLANTIC OCEAN

Gulf of Mexico

Florida (U.S.)
Tampa
Key West
(from Norfolk)
Shaffer

BAHAMA ISLANDS

Tropic of Cancer
25° N
20° N

Havana
Bahía Honda
Matanzas
Cárdenas
Isle of Pines
Cienfuegos
Júcaro

CUBA

Sampson coastal blockade
Schley coastal blockade

Great Inagua

Manzanillo
Santiago de Cuba
San Luis
Guantánamo
Daiquri
Naval battle July 3

Sampson June 1
June 20

Cervera (May 19 from Spain)

JAMAICA

Caribbean Sea

HAITI
Port-au-Prince

DOMINICAN REPUBLIC
Santo Domingo

Miles

PUERTO RICO
San Juan
Guánica July 25
Guayama

70° W
80° W

N

0   200 km
0   200 miles

the city. Meanwhile, U.S. troops are already suffering from tropical disease, heat, and inadequate food.

- *July 1:* The Americans commence their attack on the Spanish positions on the hills. One of them is dubbed "Kettle Hill" because of a large iron kettle used for sugar processing on its summit. In an attack coordinated with those on other hills, the Rough Riders dismount and rush up Kettle Hill; although they and Teddy Roosevelt will get the credit for this daring and successful attack, two African-American regiments also participate with equal courage. By the end of this day, the U.S. forces have effectively taken control of the positions surrounding Santiago and put the city under siege.
- *July 3:* The main Spanish fleet has been anchored in Santiago Harbor since May 19. Its commander, Adm. Pascual Cervera, has been reluctant to challenge what he knows is a far superior U.S. naval force blocking the harbor, but the Spanish general in charge of all Spanish forces in Cuba orders Cervera to attack. The six Spanish ships are hopelessly outgunned by the seven American ships, and within four hours they are sunk or out of commission. The Spanish suffer 474 casualties; the Americans have only one fatality.

U.S. warships under the command of Rear Admiral Sampson bombarding San Juan, Puerto Rico, in 1898. *(Library of Congress, Prints & Photographs Division [LC-USZ62-19546])*

- *July 4–17:* With the Spanish fleet destroyed, Brig. Gen. William Shafter, in charge of the forces besieging Santiago, demands that the Spanish in Santiago surrender unconditionally. As negotiations drag on, U.S. troops suffer from the heavy rains, malnutrition, and malaria. But the Spanish troops and civilians in Santiago are in even worse condition, and on July 17 the Spanish commander formally surrenders.

- *July 18:* Spanish diplomats in Paris ask the French government to arrange an armistice with the Americans. This same day, Gen. Nelson Miles is authorized to lead a U.S. force to wrest Puerto Rico from Spain.

- *July 25–31:* The first U.S. forces land near Ponce, in the southwest corner of Puerto Rico, and meet no resistance. By the end of the week, some 15,000 American troops have landed along the southern coast and are ready to march for the island's capital, San Juan.

- *July 29–31:* U.S. troops in the Philippines now number 11,000 and during the first night they take over the positions outside Manila that have been held by the Filipino insurgents. On July 31, the Spanish fire on the Americans, killing 10 and wounding 40.

- *August 8:* The Spanish commander in Manila secretly informs Dewey that he will surrender under two conditions: that the Americans stage a sham attack "for the sake of Spanish honor" and that the insurgents not be allowed to enter the city.

- *August 9:* Marching toward San Juan, Puerto Rico, the U.S. forces have their first serious engagements; American casualties are one dead and 16 wounded, while the Spanish force loses 40.

- *August 12:* Spain agrees to general U.S. terms for peace, and the French ambassador, acting for Spain, signs the agreement at the White House, but details must be further negotiated. The news reaches General Miles in Puerto Rico, and he calls a halt to all offensive operations. Within days, the American flag will be flying over most of Puerto Rico.

- *August 13:* After a sham battle (although six Americans were killed), U.S. troops move into Manila, pull down the Spanish flag, and raise the American flag. The Americans also enforce the other condition, not allowing Aguinaldo and his men to enter the city with arms.

- *August 16:* Word reaches the Americans in the Philippines that the United States and Spain had in fact agreed on the terms for peace on August 12. Because they had done so before the surrender of Manila, the status of the Philippines will remain an issue for some months.

The U.S. Thirty-eighth Infantry assemble in formation just after arriving in Manila in the Philippines in 1901. *(Library of Congress, Prints & Photographs Division [LC-USZ62-90238])*

- *October:* As the peace negotiations between the United States and Spain proceed in Paris, President McKinley is converted to the notion that the United States should take possession of the Philippines until the inhabitants are able to govern themselves.
- *December 10:* The United States and Spain sign the Treaty of Paris, formally ending the war. In addition to giving up Cuba, Puerto Rico, and Guam, Spain sells the Philippines to the United States for $20 million. The treaty will be debated hotly in the Senate, with many warning that the Philippines could be more costly than the United States bargained for.

1899

- *February 4:* Even as the U.S. Senate is debating the acquisition of the Philippines, Aguinaldo's army attacks U.S. troops, costing them 175 casualties.

- *February 6:* The Senate ratifies the treaty, 57-27, only one vote more than the required two-thirds majority. The Spanish-American War formally ends, but the war against the Filipino insurrection will drag on for three more years.

Results

In the war with Spain, the United States suffered 379 deaths in combat, but some 5,000 more troops died of disease or other noncombat causes. Spanish losses are some 1,000. In the war in the Philippines, U.S. losses are 4,234 men in combat or from disease and 2,818 wounded. It is estimated that the Filipinos lost at least 20,000 in the fighting while many more thousands of civilians were killed directly or indirectly in the war. In giving up Cuba, Puerto Rico, the Philippines, and Guam, Spain closed out some 400 years of empire while the United States is opening a new chapter in its own history.

7

WORLD WAR I

Europe had not experienced war since 1871, and most Europeans hoped that war belonged to the past and that the 20th century would bring a peaceful, more civilized age. Three things militated against this: the increase in arms production, the creation of entangling alliances between the major European powers, and the continued rise in nationalistic feeling, particularly in the Balkans. Moreover, Germany was increasingly frustrated at being denied what it believed was its rightful "place in the sun": Domestically, it is a largely landlocked nation that lacks space in which its dynamic economy and people can expand; internationally, it lacked an overseas empire for both resources and markets such as those controlled by Britain and France. All these stresses and strains came to a head in the summer of 1914.

1914

- *June 28:* Bosnia-Herzegovina belongs to the Austro-Hungarian Empire, but its Slavic people would prefer to join the adjacent nation of Serbia. When the heir to the Austro-Hungarian throne, Archduke Franz Ferdinand, visits Sarajevo, capital of Bosnia-Herzegovina, a Serbian nationalist, Gavrilo Princip, shoots and kills him and his wife. Princip and his coconspirators are arrested, but Austria demands that Serbia subdue its nationalist groups and allow Austria to participate in the trial of those complicit in the assassination. If Serbia does not comply, Austria threatens war.
- *July:* None of the Great Powers are eager for a general war, but they are pulled into it. Germany's Kaiser Wilhelm II grants a "blank

EUROPE, 1915

N

The Allies

The Central Powers

Neutral nations

NORWAY

North Sea

SWEDEN

Baltic Sea

DENMARK

UNITED KINGDOM

NETHERLANDS

London

ATLANTIC OCEAN

Moscow

GERMANY

Brussels

BELGIUM LUX.

Paris

FRANCE

RUSSIAN EMPIRE

Vienna

AUSTRIA-HUNGARY

SWITZ.

ITALY

MONTE-NEGRO

ROMANIA

Black Sea

SERBIA

BULGARIA

Sofia

ALBANIA

PORTUGAL

ANDORRA

SPAIN

GREECE

OTTOMAN EMPIRE

Mediterranean Sea

0   300 miles
0   300 km

SP. MOROCCO

ALGERIA

TUNISIA

check" go-ahead to Austrian emperor Franz-Josef. Telegrams and diplomats move back and forth throughout Europe, but the negotiations break down, and during July the various nations begin mobilizing their armed forces. On July 28, Austria declares war on Serbia. Because Serbia is its client state, Russia chooses to mobilize in its defense. Meanwhile, France and Great Britain belong to a loose defensive alliance, known as the Entente Cordiale ("cordial understanding"), with Russia, and it appears they will join in the fight.

- *August 1:* Germany declares war on Russia. France declares a general mobilization, and Germany moves troops into Luxembourg.
- *August 2:* Germany demands the right for its troops to pass through neutral Belgium, claiming that France intends to pass through to attack Germany.
- *August 3:* Belgium refuses the German demand, but German armies enter Belgium en route to France. Germany and France exchange declarations of war.
- *August 4:* Britain declares war on Germany. By now the war is between the Allied Powers (Russia, France, Belgium, Britain) and the

Central Powers (Germany, Austria-Hungary, Bulgaria). Turkey (the Ottoman Empire) will join the Central Powers on October 29, 1914; Italy will join the Allies on May 23, 1915.

- *August 4:* President Woodrow Wilson announces U.S. neutrality in the war.
- *August 19:* Wilson sends a message to the Senate saying that the "United States must be neutral in fact as well as in name. . . . We must be impartial in thought as well as in action." While exemplary in its appearance, Wilson's own neutrality is forced. As a committed Anglophile and former professor of government, he believes it imperative for the Allied Powers to win the war.
- *August 20:* Germans capture Brussels, the capital of Belgium, and begin a brutal destruction of Belgium people and property.
- *August 27–30:* German armies smash Russian opponents at the Battle of Tannenberg in East Prussia. The German victory ensures that Russia will not steamroll the Germans on the eastern front.
- *September 5–9:* French and German units fight the Battle of the Marne, northeast of Paris. The battle is touch and go, but the French

A Scottish soldier is examined at a dressing station in Belgium, 1914.
(National Archives)

hold their ground, partly because of the arrival of reinforcements brought by Parisian taxicabs. The battle ensures that Germany will not win the war on the western front quickly.

- *September–December:* Both sides on the western front make a race to the sea, intent on controlling the ports on the English Channel. By Christmas, a long series of trenches have been dug on both sides, and trench warfare will dominate for the next three years. Machine guns, barbed wire, and hand grenades give a definite advantage to those who fight defensively. The leading generals on both sides, however, will remain convinced that it is possible to break through the enemy trench lines; in the attempt to do so, both sides will lose thousands, indeed millions of lives over the next three years.
- *October 12–November 11:* The First Battle of Ypres, fought around the Belgian city of this name, ends in a stalemate.

1915

- *January 3–4:* The Germans fire shells with xylyl-bromide on the Russian forces on the eastern front, killing an estimated 1,100 Russians. It is the first major use of poison gas in modern warfare.
- *April 22:* At the start of the Second Battle of Ypres in Belgium, the Germans fire 168 tons of chlorine gas from 4,000 cylinders against their Allied opponents. It is the first use of such chemical weapons on the western front.
- *April 25–December 10:* The British land several divisions on the Gallipoli Peninsula guarding the Dardanelles with the goal of taking Turkey out of the war, but as the weeks and months pass, they suffer horrendous casualties. They start evacuating their troops on December 10 and complete the operation on January 9, 1915.
- *May 1:* New York newspapers carry both an advertisement for shipping aboard the British liner *Lusitania,* and a direct warning from the German government that neutrals who sail on British ships in the vicinity of the British Isles do so at their own risk. The *Lusitania* is the biggest passenger ship of the day.
- *May 7:* A German submarine torpedoes and sinks the *Lusitania* off the Irish coast. The Germans claim the ship was carrying munitions. Of the 1,198 civilians who go down with the ship, 128 are Americans. Among them are the multimillionaire Alfred Vanderbilt and Elbert Hubbard, known for his "A Message to Garcia" (a popular story of an enterprising American who carries a message from President McKin-

damaged, and windows are blown out in Brooklyn. The explosion is widely believed to have been caused by German agents.

- *August 29:* Congress passes the Naval Act of 1916, commonly called "Big Navy Act," which authorizes a 10-year plan to increase U.S. naval strength.
- *October 8:* A German submarine sinks five merchant ships (British, Dutch, Norwegian) off Nantucket Island, Massachusetts.
- *November 7:* Woodrow Wilson is reelected president of the United States. One of Wilson's campaign slogans was "He kept us out of war."

1917

- *January 1:* The Arabs in what will become Saudi Arabia have revolted against the Ottoman Turks, and on this day, T. E. Lawrence, a British scholar-diplomat who will become widely known as Lawrence of Arabia, is assigned to serve as liaison between the Arabs and the British supporting forces.
- *January 9:* Kaiser Wilhelm II decides to renounce the *Sussex* pledge and to commence unrestricted submarine warfare.
- *January 19:* Arthur Zimmermann, the German foreign minister, sends a coded telegram to the German ambassador in Mexico. The telegram is intercepted by British intelligence and passed on the President Wilson. The telegram contains an offer by Germany to restore to Mexico the lost territories of the American Southwest if it will make war on the United States. Wilson chooses to keep the telegram a secret.
- *January 22:* In a speech to the Senate, Wilson calls for "a peace without victory."
- *February 1:* The new German policy of unrestricted submarine warfare takes effect.
- *February 3:* The United States breaks off diplomatic relations with Germany.
- *March 1:* Wilson reveals the Zimmermann note to the American press. More Americans than ever are prepared to make war against Germany.
- *March 1–21:* German U-boats sink eight U.S. merchant ships. Wilson, realizing that he must act, calls a special session of Congress.
- *March 12–15:* An uprising in Saint Petersburg against Czar Nicholas leads to the czar's abdication. Russia soon has a new provisional government, led by Alexander Kerensky, who vows to remain in the war.

U.S. MARINES
FIRST TO FIGHT FOR DEMOCRACY
ENLIST AT

This recruitment poster demonstrates the distinction given to U.S. Marine divisions early on in the U.S. involvement in World War I. *(Library of Congress, Prints & Photographs Division [LC-USZ62-302868])*

- *April 2:* President Wilson asks Congress for a declaration of war on Germany. One of the most memorable phrases is "the world must be made safe for democracy."

- *April 4:* The Senate approves the declaration, by a vote of 82-6.
- *April 6:* The House of Representatives approves Wilson's request for a declaration of war. Fifty members vote against it—one of them is Jeannette Rankin of Montana, the first woman to serve in that body. Wilson signs the declaration.
- *April 7:* Songwriter George M. Cohan composes the song "Over There," which rapidly becomes Americans' favorite song of the war.
- *April 13:* Wilson establishes, by executive order, the Committee of Public Information (CPI). Chairman George Creel will extend his mission to all parts of American life, publicizing and promoting the war effort.
- *May:* The United States has by now enlisted more than 100 chemists in academic, industrial, and government laboratories to produce effective poison gases.

This Salvation Army poster alludes to George M. Cohan's morale-boosting war song, "Over There," to promote its relief efforts. The Salvation Army provided aid to entrenched troops. *(Library of Congress, Prints & Photographs Division [LC-USZC4-3172])*

- *May 18:* Congress approves the Selective Service as proposed by President Wilson.
- *May 19:* Herbert Hoover becomes Food Administrator for the war effort. Hoover will soon begin to issue calls for voluntary "wheatless" and "meatless" days.
- *May 26:* Gen. John "Black Jack" Pershing is named commander of the American Expeditionary Force (AEF). (His nickname comes from having commanded African-American soldiers in the American West.) Pershing is also known for his pursuit of Pancho Villa on both sides of the Mexican border.
- *June 13:* Paris explodes with joy at the arrival of General Pershing. When he visits Napoleon's tomb, Pershing is presented with one of Napoleon's swords. Impulsively, Pershing kisses it, and endears himself to the French people.
- *July:* A new Russian offensive fails dismally. Kerensky's prestige in Russia is diminished, and the new Bolshevik Party—led by V. I. Lenin—starts to gain ground.
- *July 4:* A small group of American soldiers in Paris march to the cemetery where the marquis de Lafayette is buried. Lt. Col. Charles Stanton, a quartermaster, there declares, "Lafayette, we are here!"
- *July 15:* Congress passes the Espionage Act. Two thousand cases will be prosecuted under the act during the war's duration.
- *July 20:* Blindfolded, the U.S. secretary of war draws the first number for the draft—258—from a large glass jar.
- *October:* Led by Lenin and Leon Trotsky, Russian Bolsheviks overthrow the provisional government. Lenin proceeds to establish the first Communist government seen anywhere, thereby drawing the alarm of Allied conservatives. Trotsky announces his plan of "No War, No Peace" with the Germans. Trotsky intends neither to prosecute the war nor to sign a treaty with Germany.
- *October 24–November 10:* The Italians have come close to defeating the Austrians during eleven battles along the Isonzo River in northeast Italy. Now the Germans provide reinforcements to the Austrians and they launch an offensive near Caporetto, north of Trieste. Caught off guard, the Italians suffer heavy casualties as they retreat all the way to the Piave River, northeast of Venice.
- *November 2:* Three Americans are killed and 11 are captured by a German raiding party at Artois, France. Cpl. James Gresham, Pvt.

Merle Hay, and Pvt. Thomas Enright are later honored as the first enlisted men to be killed in action on the western front.

- *November 20:* The Battle of Cambrai begins in France. No Americans are involved in this, the first battle where tanks are used in a group. Three hundred twenty-four Mark IV British tanks go into battle. Slow and prone to breakdowns, they do not appear as instant winners.

- *November–December:* Germany responds to Trotsky's policy of "No war, no peace," by pressing deep into Russia and taking more territory.

1918

- *January 8:* Wilson outlines his Fourteen Points before a joint session of Congress. The points include calls for a resurrected Poland, freedom of the seas, and an end to all secret diplomacy and treaties ("open covenants, openly arrived at"). Public response is overwhelmingly positive. Wilson succeeds in capturing the moral high ground.

- *March 3:* At Brest-Litovsk, Russian commissioners sign a treaty that yields one-third of European Russia to Germany. This punitive treaty gives Germany breathing room on the eastern front, but it also alerts other nations what they may expect if Germany is victorious. Immediately following the treaty, German divisions are transferred from the Russian to the western front.

- *March 21:* German general Erich von Ludendorff launches an offensive in the Somme region, north of Paris. He gambles that his sledgehammer blows will cave in the Allied defenses before the Americans reach the scene.

- *April 24:* The only battle between tanks in the war takes place near Amiens, France. Australian units supported by three or four tanks throw back a German attack with an equal number of tanks.

- *April 29:* American captain Eddie Rickenbacher and Capt. James Hall down a German plane. It is Rickenbacher's first "kill" and only the fourth for the United States so far. About a month later, he changes his name to "Rickenbacker" to avoid being connected with his Swiss-German heritage. By the end of the war, Rickenbacker will have shot down 26 German airplanes.

- *May:* The United States establishes the Chemical Warfare Service, and during the summer the U.S. Army will establish a unit in France that will occasionally fire various poison gases at the Germans.

- *May 20:* Wilson signs the Overton Act. The act gives the president authority to coordinate or consolidate executive offices in any way he

Three soldiers from the Ninth Machine Gun Battalion photographed in a railroad shop in Château-Thierry, June 1918. *(National Archives)*

sees fit in the prosecution of the war. Constitutional historians have seen this as potentially a dangerous piece of legislation, but Wilson will use it sparingly.

- *June 1:* A U.S. machine gun unit joins French units in the defense of Château-Thierry, just northeast of Paris.
- *June 4:* Ernest Hemingway's service as a Red Cross driver in Italy begins. He is one of many Americans—some of whom will become notable figures later on—who serve as ambulance drivers. Among them are E. E. Cummings, Archibald MacLeish, Walt Disney, and Ray Kroc, founder of McDonald's.
- *June 6–26:* U.S. Marine units stop a German attack at Belleau Wood, not far north of Paris. The marines suffer 7,000 casualties and earn the name "Devil Dogs" from the Germans.
- *July 1:* American troops attack and take Vaux, near Château-Thierry.
- *July 8:* Ernest Hemingway is wounded by an Austrian mortar shell. He spends several months at the Red Cross hospital in Milan; he will use this experience in his novel *Farewell to Arms* (1929).
- *July 10:* Six fully loaded U.S. American bombers, low on gas, land in Koblenz, Germany. It is the largest single surrender of American

aircraft during the war. German propaganda makes much of this event.

- *July 14:* Quentin Roosevelt, youngest son of former president Theodore Roosevelt, is shot down and killed near the village of Chamery, France. The German airmen bury him with military honors.
- *July 18:* The Allied Forces (French, British, and American) go on the offensive all along the western front. Unlike other such beginnings, this one will not prove to be a false start, and day by day they drive the Germans back.
- *August 26:* German units start to retreat to the Hindenburg Line, which the Germans call the Siegfried Line. Rather than a wall, it is a four-layer defensive network northeast of Paris. General Von Ludendorff refers to this as the "Black Day" of the German army.
- *August 30:* French Marshal Foch visits General Pershing at his headquarters. Foch wants to break up the U.S. Army to serve in piecemeal segments with the French and British. Pershing absolutely refuses. He asks Foch to grant him a sector, any sector of the front, but insists that the Americans must fight as one. Foch soon grants Pershing the Meuse-Argonne sector.
- *September:* The first outbreak of influenza (later called the Spanish flu) appears in the United States. It begins in army camps and navy bases, and spreads rapidly to the civilian population.
- *September 1:* By now there are more than 1 million U.S. troops in France.
- *September 11:* Some 4,500 U.S. soldiers land at Archangel on the northwest coast of Russia. They are part of an Allied force intended to prevent a Bolshevik victory in the ongoing civil war between the White (pro-Czarist) and Red (Bolshevik) Russians. The U.S. part in this intervention will long be remembered in Russia.
- *September 12–13:* The U.S. First Army begins its attack against the St. Mihiel salient. This is the first offensive conducted solely by Americans in the war, and they thoroughly rout the Germans.
- *September 26:* The U.S. First Army begins the Meuse-Argonne offensive in the region east of Verdun, near the Luxembourg border. This is one of the largest operations of the war. French and Italian units move out of the way, according to plan, and U.S. units take their place. The entire offensive, involving the movement of about 1 million men, is directed by U.S. colonel George Marshall.

- *September 29:* After a disastrous defeat of its army in Macedonia, Bulgaria, one of the Central Powers, drops out of the war.
- *October:* The Spanish flu (influenza) pandemic worsens dramatically. One the worst day, 800 people die in Philadelphia. Hardest hit are those cities that are close to army and navy bases. Some 500,000 Americans will die before the pandemic abates in April 1919.
- *October 1:* Combined Arab and British forces enter Damascus, Syria. Accompanying them is Lawrence of Arabia, widely credited for his courageous and inspiring leadership during the 21-month campaign to drive the Turks out of their empire which includes the Arabian Peninsula and the Near East.
- *October 1–8:* In the Argonne Forest, a battalion of 600 New Yorkers finds itself trapped by Germans in a valley. Dubbed "The Lost Battalion," by the time they are relieved, only 194 survive.
- *October 4–30:* The second phase of the Meuse-Argonne offensive. By now the Americans are making gains all along the line.

A German aviator drops a bomb somewhere on the western front. In spite of German efforts, the Allies are steadily pushing the western front eastward.
(National Archives)

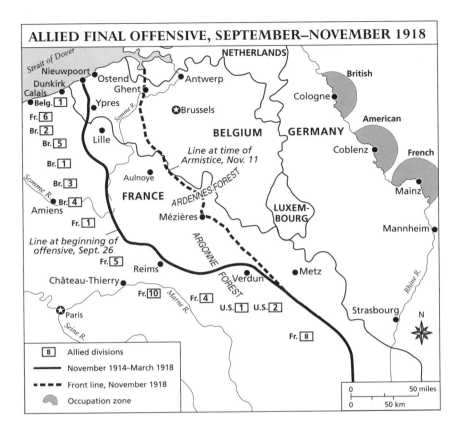

ALLIED FINAL OFFENSIVE, SEPTEMBER–NOVEMBER 1918

- *October 6:* Prince Max of Baden, newly appointed German chancellor by the kaiser, initiates peace negotiations through intermediaries in Switzerland. Max appeals to President Wilson to seek a peace based on the Fourteen Points.
- *October 8:* Cpl. Alvin York outshoots an entire German machine gun battalion; he silences 35 guns and kills about 17 men. York and his depleted squad of nine men then capture about 132 German prisoners. York will receive the Medal of Honor and decorations from most of the Allied nations. When drafted, York had asked to be a conscientious objector: the request was denied.
- *October 10:* A German submarine torpedoes a British passenger ship off the Irish coast; 292 lives are lost. This effectively ends the peace discussions between Prince Max and President Wilson, who now declares that Germany will have to accept the terms of the Allied military.

- *October 29:* German sailors mutiny at Kiel. Their commanders had urged them to make a suicidal venture out of the harbor to attack British ships. German soldiers sent to suppress the mutiny join the sailors and rebellion spreads.
- *October 30:* Realizing that the Central Powers were on the verge of defeat, Turkey drops out of the war.
- *November 1:* The largest U.S. ground force up to that time sent to battle joins with the French in an offensive along the Meuse River.
- *November 4:* Austria-Hungary signs an armistice with the Allied Powers. Kaiser Wilhelm's top military leaders inform him the struggle is at an end.
- *November 9:* Germany declares that the German Empire is at an end. The new German Republic is proclaimed.
- *November 10:* Kaiser Wilhelm II abdicates and goes into exile in Holland.
- *November 11:* At 5 A.M., French and German representatives sign an armistice in a railroad car at Compiègne, France. Hostilities end at 11 A.M.

1919

- *January–May:* In Paris, Wilson negotiates with Georges Clemenceau of France, Lloyd George of Britain, and Vittorio Orlando of Italy. Wilson's dearest wish is to have the clause that establishes the new League of Nations in the treaty. He obtains this clause but has to agree to the French desire to punish Germany with reparations, and to the British and French desire to retain their colonial empires. They do so under a new system of mandates, intended to prepare colonial peoples around the world for eventual self-rule.
- *June 28:* Germany is forced to sign the Treaty of Versailles, named after the great palace outside Paris where the ceremony takes place.
- *July 10:* Wilson, recently returned home, presents the Versailles Treaty to the Senate. He expresses the view that the treaty is essential to the well-being of the United States and the world. A group of senators, led by Henry Cabot Lodge, oppose the clause that would require the United States to aid France in the event of a future German invasion.
- *September:* Facing Senate resistance, Wilson goes on a speaking tour. He travels by railway car, giving speeches about the import-

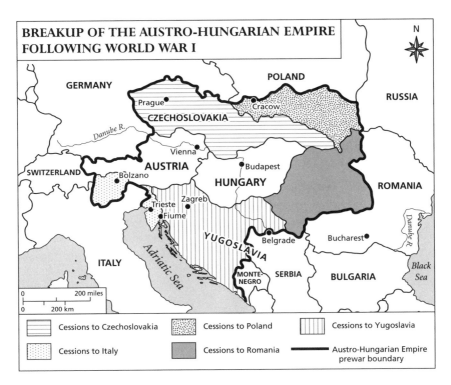

ance of the treaty. Wilson collapses in Pueblo, Colorado, from exhaustion.

- *October 2:* Back in Washington, D.C., Wilson suffers a stroke that leaves him disabled. For the next year, his wife will limit access to the invalid president. Any compromise between Wilson and his Senate opponents is out of the question.
- *November 19:* The U.S. Senate rejects the Versailles Treaty. It will do so again on March 19, 1920.

Results

Exact casualty figures for both sides are not known, but the best estimates are that some 11,000,000 were killed in combat, while another 21,000,000 were wounded—many of these so seriously that they would suffer for the rest of their lives. Germany, Russia, and Austria-Hungary lost the most personnel; France and Great Britain (including their colonial forces) also lost large numbers; so, too, did Italy. Civilian deaths are estimated at between 5 million and 10 million. Of these figures, U.S. losses were some 50,000 killed in action and another 200,000 wounded in action. Disease killed another 63,000 U.S. military personnel. The cost in money is incalculable: Direct costs alone have been estimated at $7 trillion in 2002 dollars. Yet even these figures would be surpassed by those of World War II, which most historians agree grew directly out of the Versailles Treaty's punitive treatment of Germany: It not only assigned all the blame for the war on Germany, took away about 13 percent of Germany's land, and eliminated its entire navy and most of its army, it made Germany pay reparations of some $33 billion. It is not difficult to see how Adolf Hitler later used the Treaty of Versailles as an effective piece of propaganda, convincing the Germans they needed a strong leader to overcome the hardships imposed by the treaty and to restore their nation to its rightful place among the world's powers. The only country to emerge strengthened from the war was the United States: With its homeland untouched, relatively few casualties, and newly developed manufacturing capacity, the United States appeared ready to assume a major role in world affairs but, by refusing to join the League of Nations, it left other nations to go down the road that led to World War II.

8

WORLD WAR II

In 1933, Adolf Hitler became chancellor of Germany and Franklin D. Roosevelt (hereafter referred to as FDR) became president of the United States. FDR and many Americans watched with mounting concern as Hitler and his Nazi Party suppressed all internal opposition and then turned their military on Germany's neighbors. Appealing to the abuses of the 1919 Treaty of Versailles, Hitler took the Rhineland (1936) and Austria (1937). Meanwhile, Italy's Fascist dictator, Benito Mussolini, moved into Albania (1934) and Ethiopia (1935–36). During these same years, Japan flexed its muscles and moved to obtain the natural resources of its neighbors. Japan took over Manchuria as early as 1931, and by the end of 1938 Japan controlled much of eastern China. At the same time, the Japanese encountered a new threat from Soviet Russia, which felt its eastern coastline endangered by the Japanese expansion. On November 24, 1936, Germany and Japan signed the Anti-Comintern Pact; Italy would sign on November 6, 1937. Ostensibly, these three countries were united in their opposition to the spread of communism, but they were in fact bent on their own expansion.

1938

- *September 30:* Hitler has been threatening to take over the ethnic German region of Czechoslovakia known as the Sudetenland. The prime ministers of Britain and France, Neville Chamberlain and Edouard Daladier, meet Hitler and Mussolini in Munich, Germany, and on this day agree to let Hitler do this. Chamberlain flies home announcing that they have guaranteed "peace in our time."

1939

- *March:* Germany, Hungary, and Poland divide up what is left of Czechoslovakia.
- *July 26:* The United States abrogates its commercial treaty with Japan to show its disapproval of Japan's treatment of China.
- *August:* Hitler has now turned against Poland. German planes drop leaflets on Poland urging Poles to join the German nation.
- *August 20–31:* Soviet Marshal Zhukov uses a classic double envelopment to inflict 60,000 casualties upon the Japanese at the Battle of Khalkin-Gol in Manchuria. This little-known battle will allow Stalin to bring troops home from the East and to concentrate on his new agreement with Adolf Hitler.
- *August 23:* Nazi and Soviet foreign ministers sign a non-aggression pact while dividing up parts of eastern Europe and the Baltic states. The agreement comes as a complete surprise to the democratic powers of Britain and France. Hitler and Stalin have always seen each other as deadly rivals: Now they have come to terms, allowing Hitler a free hand for his planned aggressions.
- *September 1:* German troops, tanks, and planes attack Poland. The Poles fight bravely but are outmatched in every category.
- *September 3:* Britain and France declare war on Germany, but it comes too late to save Poland. Nevertheless, some members of the German leadership are dismayed. They had believed that they could persuade Britain at least to stay out of the war.
- *September 3:* FDR announces U.S. neutrality. He cautions however that he cannot expect Americans to be neutral in their thoughts.
- *September 4:* Japan declares neutrality in the European war. Japan has its hands full with its own war with China.
- *September 10:* Canada declares war on Germany.
- *September 17:* Soviet dictator Joseph Stalin sends his troops against eastern Poland. Stalin does not want Hitler to obtain all of the spoils.
- *October:* A letter composed by physicist Albert Einstein is delivered to FDR; in it, Einstein warns that it is possible to make a weapon in which nuclear chain reactions could cause horrendous damage, and because the Germans may try to make such a weapon, the United States must consider doing so, too.
- *October 1:* By this date, Poland has ceased to exist. The Germans have taken the western two-thirds, and Russia has taken the eastern third.

German troops parade through Warsaw, Poland, in September 1939.
(National Archives)

- *November 30–December 31:* The Soviet Army invades neighboring Finland. The smaller nation had refused a set of demands made upon it, including a Russian demand to use Finnish land for military training purposes. Russia has all the advantages in men and materials, but the Finns fight courageously and inflict some humiliating defeats on the Russians.
- *December 14:* The Soviet Union is expelled from the League of Nations because of its unprovoked attack on Finland.

1940

- *January–April:* Because no major action occurs on either side, many people call this time the "Phony War." It appears as if neither the Germans nor their enemies truly want to engage in a major campaign.

- *March 13:* Russia and Finland sign a peace treaty. Finland is punished with a loss of territory but remains an independent nation. About 200,000 Russians have died in the war, leading other nations to the erroneous conclusion that Russia is an easy enemy to fight.
- *April 9:* German forces invade Norway. Its long coastline will provide advantages to the Germans in submarine warfare.
- *May 10:* German forces invade Belgium, Holland, and Luxembourg. On the same day, Winston Churchill replaces Neville Chamberlain as British prime minister.
- *May 12:* The Germans invade France. Meeting little resistance, they will take Paris by June 14.
- *May 26–June 4:* The British—using civilian boats as well as Royal Navy vessels—evacuate the bulk of their army from Dunkirk, France. The last British units cross just hours before German forces arrive on the beaches. Some 338,226 troops have been evacuated. The British hail the miracle of Dunkirk, but Churchill cautions that wars are not won through retreats, however ingenious.
- *June:* Hitler makes overtures of peace toward Britain. He declares in a speech to the Reichstag that "I see no reason why this war must go on." The offer is spurned by Churchill. Hitler begins to plan Operation Sea Lion, his invasion of England.
- *June 10:* Mussolini brings Italy into the war as a German ally.
- *June 22:* Hitler signs the armistice with France in the same railway car at Compiègne in which Germany signed the World War I armistice on November 11, 1918. The Germans will occupy the northern half of France but leave the southern half under a puppet government based in Vichy. A small number of French—led by Charles de Gaulle—go into exile and become known as the "Free French."
- *July 10:* German fighters and bombers commence serious bombing raids on Britain, thus starting the air war that will become known as the Battle of Britain.
- *September 7:* Although he has made headway against the British airfields, Hitler now turns his attention on the major cities. The "London Blitz" begins this day.
- *September 16:* FDR signs the Selective Training and Service Act. All men between 21 and 35 must register for military training.
- *September 27:* Germany, Italy, and Japan sign the Tripartite Pact, in which they vow to defend one another against Allied attacks.

- *October 12:* Hitler abandons preparations for Operation Sea Lion, the planned invasion of Great Britain. His generals continue to plan for a resumption the following spring, but Hitler already has thoughts about attacking the Soviet Union.
- *October 28–November 16:* Mussolini's forces invade northern Greece on October 28, but the Greeks, aided by the British air force, push the Italians back into Albania by November 16.
- *October 29:* The U.S. secretary of war draws the first number— 158—in the draft lottery.
- *October 31:* Hitler has effectively lost the Battle of Britain in the air. A few hundred Royal Air Force (RAF) pilots have defeated the Germans in the skies, even though thousands of bombs are dropped on London, Coventry, and other British cities.
- *November 5:* FDR wins reelection for what will be his third term. One of FDR's campaign statements was, "Your boys are not going to be sent into any foreign wars."
- *December 29:* In one of his "fireside chats"—really radio addresses —FDR says, "We must be the great arsenal of democracy."

1941

- *January 6:* In his State of the Union address, FDR defines what he calls the Four Freedoms: freedom of speech, freedom of expression, freedom from want, and freedom from fear. There is little doubt where FDR's sympathies lie in the war between the Allied Powers and Germany, but polls reveal that about half of all Americans still support neutrality.
- *January:* Japanese admiral Isokoru Yamamoto makes the first secret proposal for a carrier-borne attack on Pearl Harbor, Hawaii. Although he recognizes the great industrial strength of the United States, Yamamoto believes that rifts in American society will prevent the United States from striking back effectively.
- *February:* German general Erwin Rommel arrives in North Africa. He organizes the German units there into the Afrika Korps and will become known as one of the most daring and charismatic of the German military leaders.
- *February 4:* The United Service Organizations (USO) is established to provide social support for the increasingly numerous and far-flung U.S. military personnel.

- *March 11:* FDR signs the Lend-Lease Bill, under which the United States lends Britain American war matériel; in exchange, Britain lends naval and air bases in the Western Hemisphere to U.S. forces. It is a thinly disguised way to aid Britain, and gradually the program will provide aid of all kinds to the Allies.
- *April:* A. Philip Randolph, leader of the Brotherhood of Sleeping Car Porters union, plans a massive march on Washington to demonstrate African-Americans' dissatisfaction with their status in society. To forestall the event, FDR issues an executive order that establishes the Fair Employment Practices Commission.
- *May:* British naval and air units find the German battleship *Bismarck* near the French coast and sink it.
- *May–June:* Hitler has to bail his Italian ally, Benito Mussolini, out of a troubled invasion of Greece. This costs Hitler a valuable six weeks.
- *May–June:* British intelligence sends numerous warnings to Soviet Russia that Germany is massing troops and tanks on the border. Stalin ignores the warnings.
- *May 20–June 1:* German paratroopers and glider-borne troops capture the island of Crete, but the victory is costly in terms of skilled personnel and Hitler vows not to repeat such an operation.
- *May 27:* FDR declares an unlimited state of emergency, in response to the German conquest of Greece and Yugoslavia.
- *June 14:* FDR freezes the assets of Germany and Italy in the United States.
- *June 22:* Operation Barbarossa, the German invasion of Soviet Russia, begins. Hitler announces the invasion to the German Reichstag: "The world will hold its breath." Only now do some of those who have read *Mein Kampf* recall that Hitler had written that Germany needed *Lebensraum* ("living space") that could only be found on the steppes of Russia.
- *July–September:* The Germans make immense gains in Russia. Perhaps 3 million Russians are killed, and as many others are taken prisoner during these first months.
- *July 7:* U.S. Marines land in Iceland. FDR has promised that the United States will defend that island against any German attacks.
- *July 24:* Imperial Japan invades Indochina, which has been a French colony since the 1860s.
- *August 1:* FDR forbids the export of oil and aviation fuel from the United States to Japan. Japanese military leaders immediately

WAR IN EUROPE, 1941–1942

Axis powers	1 1941–42 British and Axis forces battle across desert	7 Dec. 5,1941–April 1942 Russian counter-offensive
Allied with Axis	2 April 6–17, 1941 German invasion of Yugoslavia	8 Oct. 23–Nov. 4, 1942 Battle of El Alamein
Occupied by Germany	3 April 6–28, 1941 German invasion of Greece	9 November 8, 1942 Allied landings in North Africa
Vichy French	4 May 20–29, 1941 Invasion of Crete	10 November 9, 1942 German landings in Tunisia
Allied counter-offensives	5 June 22, 1941 Operation Barbarossa: Germany invades Russia	11 November 11, 1942 Germany occupies Vichy France
Neutral powers	6 September 15, 1941 Leningrad besieged	12 November 19, 1942 Russian counter-offensive

set in motion plans for a preemptive strike against the United
States.

- *August 11:* FDR and Winston Churchill meet for the first time
aboard the USS *Augusta,* anchored off Newfoundland. The two—

both former naval leaders—strike it off well. They compose the Atlantic Charter, a statement in favor of democratic leadership around the world.

- *August 18:* FDR signs the Selective Service Act extension, which removes the previous limit of 900,000 men to be selected.
- *August 28:* The German Army Group North begins its assault on Leningrad.
- *September:* The Germans capture the city of Kiev in the Ukraine. It is a tremendous victory, but the effort expended here has cost part of the precious months needed to reach Moscow.
- *September 15–January 27, 1944:* The German army keeps the city of Leningrad under siege. Although it produces horrible conditions for the people of Leningrad, the fact that they hold out becomes an inspiration to many and ties down large elements of the German army.
- *September 16:* The U.S. Navy announces it will defend all shipping in the Atlantic as far east as Iceland. This is a blow to the Germans, who have been wreaking havoc with their U-boat campaign.
- *October:* Charles Lindbergh, first person to fly across the Atlantic alone, makes an impassioned speech in Des Moines, Iowa. Lindbergh, who is already known as a supporter of the "America First" isolationist movement, now attacks Jews and bankers, claiming they want to drag America into the war.
- *October 17:* The U.S. destroyer *Kearny* is torpedoed off Iceland. The ship does not sink, but 11 Americans are killed.
- *October 27:* FDR announces that "America has been attacked, the shooting has started." He holds back from asking for an actual declaration of war.
- *October 31:* A U-boat sinks the U.S. destroyer *Reuben James.* One hundred Americans are killed. FDR soon gives permission for navy ships to shoot on sight.
- *November 26:* Six Japanese aircraft carriers, two battleships, and a group of smaller vessels leave Japan and head for Hawaii. The task force maintains complete radio silence.
- *December 5:* Advance German units enter a suburb of Moscow, barely 20 miles from the Kremlin. The weather in and around Moscow turns sharply for the worse. It is 40 degrees below zero, and the German tanks will not start. The Germans are suffering; Hitler

had anticipated the campaign would be won by now, and few of his men have winter uniforms.

- *December 6:* Russian units attack all along the line in front of Moscow. Many of the Russians have been brought in from Siberia; they have excellent winter clothing, skis, and even snowshoes. Stung by the first Russian counterattack in months, the Germans fall back.
- *December 6:* FDR makes a personal appeal to Emperor Hirohito for peace. FDR relishes personal diplomacy, but this time he has been outfoxed.
- *December 7:* Planes are launched by the Japanese task force that left Japan on November 26. Japanese pilots strike the U.S. naval base at Pearl Harbor, Hawaii, without warning. Seven battleships are damaged or destroyed, but the U.S. aircraft carriers are out at sea and are unharmed. First shock, then anger spreads throughout the United States as news of the attack comes in over the radio.
- *December 8:* Roosevelt labels December 7 as "a date which will live in infamy." He asks for and receives a declaration of war on Japan. The one dissenting vote in the House of Representatives comes from Jeannette Rankin, who also voted against entering World War I.
- *December 9:* Japanese planes attack American planes on the ground in the Philippines. The loss of planes puts Gen. Douglas MacArthur completely on the defensive.
- *December 10:* The island of Guam falls to the Japanese.
- *December 10:* Japanese planes find, attack, and sink two major British battleships, the *Prince of Wales* and *Repulse* in the South China Sea.
- *December 11:* Hitler declares war on the United States. The United States now faces a war on two oceans and two fronts.
- *December 19:* Hitler assumes personal control of all Germany army operations. On the eastern front he demands that his troops fight for every yard, every inch.
- *December 22:* Winston Churchill and his staff arrive in Washington, D.C., for meetings that will be called the Arcadia Conference. One of the resolutions of the conference will be "Germany First." Hitler and the Nazis are seen as the greatest danger.
- *December 22:* Wake Island falls to the Japanese.
- *December 25:* The Japanese capture British Hong Kong.

Even without recruitment posters like this, there would have been a rush of enlistees after the attack on Pearl Harbor. *(National Archives)*

1942

- *January 2:* Manila falls to the Japanese.
- *January 20:* At a villa at Wannsee in Berlin, various Nazi leaders convene and agree on a protocol that expressly confirms the process of a "final solution" to the "problem" of Jews in Europe—namely, their liquidation.
- *February 15:* The British garrison at Singapore surrenders to the Japanese. Suddenly, a Japanese invasion of Australia appears quite possible.
- *February 20:* FDR authorizes the removal of Japanese Americans from their homes along the West Coast to internment camps in the

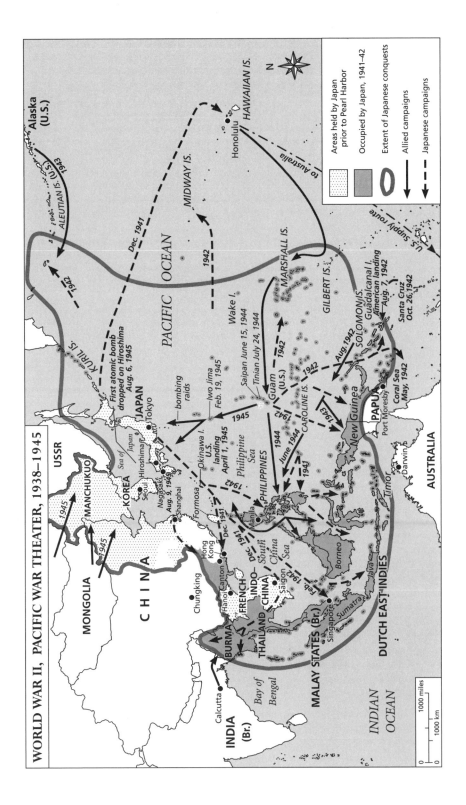

WORLD WAR II, PACIFIC WAR THEATER, 1938–1945

Legend:
- Areas held by Japan prior to Pearl Harbor
- Occupied by Japan, 1941–42
- Extent of Japanese conquests
- Allied campaigns
- Japanese campaigns

N

Locations and labels:

Alaska (U.S.)

ALEUTIAN IS. (U.S.) 1943

USSR

MONGOLIA

MANCHUKUO 1945

KOREA
- Seoul
- 1945

CHINA
- Chungking
- Shanghai

JAPAN
- Tokyo
- Hiroshima, Aug. 6, 1945
- Nagasaki, Aug. 9, 1945

First atomic bomb dropped on Hiroshima Aug. 6, 1945

Sea of Japan

KURIL IS.

Dec. 1941

1942

1942

PACIFIC OCEAN

MIDWAY IS. 1942

HAWAIIAN IS.
- Honolulu

to Australia

Wake I.

MARSHALL IS.

GILBERT IS.

Iwo Jima Feb. 19, 1945

bombing raids

1945

Saipan June 15, 1944
Tinian July 24, 1944

Guam (U.S.) 1942

Okinawa I. U.S. landing April 1, 1945

Formosa

Philippine Sea

PHILIPPINES
- Manila

1944

June 1944

CAROLINE IS. 1942

1943

1942

Aug 1942

SOLOMON IS.
Guadalcanal I. American landing Aug. 7, 1942

Santa Cruz Oct. 26, 1942

New Guinea

PAPUA
- Port Moresby

Coral Sea May, 1942

AUSTRALIA

Darwin

Hanoi
Canton Dec. 1941

Hong Kong

FRENCH INDO-CHINA
- Saigon

THAILAND

BURMA

South China Sea

Borneo

Feb. 1942

Timor

DUTCH EAST INDIES

Java

Sumatra

Singapore

MALAY STATES (Br.)

INDIA (Br.)
- Calcutta

Bay of Bengal

INDIAN OCEAN

U.S. Supply route

0   1000 miles
0   1000 km

American West. About 110,000 people will eventually suffer from this decision. No such action is taken against Germans on the East Coast or in the Midwest.

- *February 27–March 1:* Japan wins the naval Battle of the Java Sea.
- *March 11:* General MacArthur leaves the Philippines, saying, "I shall return."
- *April 9:* 12,000 U.S. and 63,000 Filipino soldiers surrender to the Japanese at Bataan in the Philippines.
- *April 10:* The Bataan Death March begins at dawn. American and Filipino prisoners are forced to march 85 miles in six days, with only one significant meal the entire time. Thousands die from lack of water.
- *April 18:* Lt. Col. James Doolittle leads 16 B-52 bombers from the carrier USS *Hornet* to the home islands of Japan. Doolittle's pilots drop bombs on five major Japanese cities, then continue to China, where most of the crews survive; two planes, however, land in Japan-

This picture, captured from the Japanese, shows U.S. prisoners using improvised litters to carry those comrades who, from lack of food or water on the march from Bataan, fell along the road, in 1942.
(National Archives)

An army B-25 takes off from the deck of the USS *Hornet* to take part in the first U.S. air raid on Japan, the Doolittle Raid in April 1942. *(National Archives)*

ese-occupied China and three of the crew are executed. The daring raid lifts American spirits, and convinces top Japanese leaders to seek out a major carrier-to-carrier battle in the Pacific.

- *May:* American lieutenant Joseph Rochefort, working 16-hour days at Pearl Harbor, succeeds in partially breaking the Japanese naval code. He alerts naval commanders that a massive Japanese war fleet is due to leave the home islands soon. The commanders decide that the Midway Islands are the most likely target.
- *May 2–8:* The Battle of the Coral Sea. U.S. and Japanese fleets fight a long battle in the Coral Sea. The climactic battle is fought on May 8. This is the first battle in recorded history where two fleets fight without ever seeing each other; their fighters and bombers do the work. It is not a decisive battle, but the Americans do well enough that the Japanese have to turn aside from their drive toward Australia.
- *May 6:* Gen. Jonathan Wainwright surrenders the fortress of Corregidor, Philippines, to the Japanese.
- *June:* The Germans seize the initiative on the Russian front. Major German forces aim south and west, toward the oil fields in the

Caucasus Mountains region. One of the clear obstacles in their path is Stalingrad.

- *June 3–4:* A great air battle takes place over and around the Midway Islands. Japanese admiral Yamamoto has assembled a massive Japanese fleet, with superiority of numbers, but the advantage of surprise has been lost. The Japanese and American fleets are never in sight of one another; they exchange waves of fighters and bombers. The Americans prevail late in the day. U.S. planes descend from the clouds and create havoc with Japanese planes ready to take off. The Japanese lose four aircraft carriers and limp homeward. Yamamoto knows that Japan has lost its chance for a quick end to the war.

- *June 17:* The first issue of *Yank* is published. The army-sponsored newspaper will soon become a favorite with G.I.'s.

- *June 21:* German general Rommel captures Tobruk in North Africa. The way is now open for him to advance east toward the oil fields in Egypt.

- *June 27:* A convoy of 35 merchant ships—22 of them American—leaves Iceland, bound for the Arctic coast of Russia. By the time the convoy reaches Murmansk, 24 of the ships are sunk by German planes

The USS *Lexington* as it exploded during the Battle of the Coral Sea, May 7–8, 1942. *(Library of Congress, Prints & Photographs Division [LC-USZ62-122774])*

Heavy rains often made roads impassable in Guadalcanal, 1942. *(Library of Congress, Prints & Photographs Division [LC-USZ62-106359])*

and U-boats. This is one of the greatest successes for the German U-boat campaign.

- *July 6:* In Amsterdam, a young girl named Anne Frank, her mother, father, and sister, go into hiding in a secret annex in her father's office building; they will soon be joined by four other Jews who, like the Franks, fear that the Germans will send them off to concentration camps. Anne will keep a diary throughout their stay in the annex.
- *August:* The Japanese High Command makes the decision to fight for Guadalcanal.
- *August 7:* U.S. Marines land on the island of Guadalcanal in the Solomon Islands. They seize the beginnings of an airstrip that the Japanese had constructed.
- *August 19:* British and Canadian troops make a raid on Dieppe, a port city in northern France. The raid ends in disaster; 3,600 Allied troops are lost along with 106 aircraft. This failure will deter many British planners from accepting the eventual Operation Overlord plan for the invasion of France.
- *September:* Rommel and his Afrika Korps run out of gasoline and out of momentum in the eastern part of Egypt.

A 105mm howitzer is towed along the Algerian beach. Troopships can be seen in the background. *(Library of Congress, Prints & Photographs Division [LC-USZ62-98937])*

- *September 3:* Advance units of the German Sixth Army reach the outskirts of Stalingrad. German commander General von Paulus expects a quick takeover, but the Russians put up fierce resistance. The house-to-house fighting that follows is a war of attrition that favors the Russians.
- *September 13:* Japanese soldiers attack in waves on Guadalcanal, shouting "Banzai" and "Marine you die!" The Americans hold their position.
- *October 23–November 4:* British general Montgomery leads the British in the Second Battle of El-Alamein in Egypt. Operating carefully, drawing on superior numbers and mobility, Montgomery forces Rommel back.
- *November–December:* The Battle for Guadalcanal continues.
- *November 8–13:* American troops, led by Gen. Dwight Eisenhower, land in French North Africa. The Vichy French forces put up a token fight before yielding in the next 10 days. This "Operation Torch" is the first major American effort on the European/North African front. Rommel is now trapped between the British in Egypt and the Americans to his west.
- *November 12:* The United States lowers the draft age from 21 to 18.

- *November 19:* Russian marshal Zhukov launches a massive counteroffensive that traps the German Sixth Army in and around Stalingrad. The Germans have chances to fight their way out, but any such action is forbidden by Hitler. The Führer has been led astray by Field Marshal Göring, who insists that the German air force can resupply the men at Stalingrad by air.

1943

- *January:* German U-boat strength is at its peak: 212 vessels, with the majority placed in the North Atlantic.
- *January 14–23:* FDR and Churchill meet at Casablanca, North Africa. They formulate the demand for an unconditional surrender by the Axis Powers—nothing less will be accepted. Some will later criticize the decision, arguing that the hard stance prolonged the war.
- *January 31:* Field Marshal Von Paulus and what remains of the German Sixth Army surrender at Stalingrad. Hitler is disappointed; he had awarded von Paulus a field marshal's baton just hours earlier, hoping that von Paulus would honor precedent and commit suicide (no Prussian field marshal was ever taken alive until this time). Of the 90,000 Germans who survive and go into captivity, only about 5,000 will ever see home again.
- *February 9:* The last Japanese resistance on Guadalcanal comes to an end. The United States has suffered 1,752 men killed; the Japanese dead are calculated at 24,000.
- *February 14–20:* The Battle of Kasserine Pass in North Africa. The German Tiger tank proves superior to the U.S. Sherman tank. Rommel and the Afrika Korps keep the Americans back and inflict about 1,000 casualties.
- *March 9:* Rommel departs from North Africa for the last time. He knows that the men he leaves behind are doomed to either death or capture by the Allies.
- *March 9:* The Russian people learn—via radio—that their country is receiving supplies from Britain and the United States. It is the first time that Stalin's regime has made this information public, even though assistance has been coming in since fall 1941.
- *March 16–19:* Thirty-eight U-boats converge on two Allied convoys off the east coast of Newfoundland. Twenty-one merchant ships, which displace 141,000 tons, are destroyed at the cost of only one

U-boat. It is the high point of success for the Germans in the North Atlantic.

- *March 21:* Mud from the spring thaw brings the campaign in Russia to a temporary halt.
- *April 1:* Food rationing begins in the United States.
- *April 18:* Japanese admiral Yamamoto is killed when his airplane is shot down over Bougainville Island. Thanks to the fact they could read the Japanese code, the U.S. military knew he was in that plane.
- *April 18:* Over the Mediterranean, 51 German transport planes, carrying supplies to the beleaguered forces in Tunisia, are shot down in the space of half an hour. Allied pilots call it the "Palm Sunday Shoot."
- *April 19:* The massacre of Jews in the Warsaw Ghetto begins, as part of Hitler's "Final Solution."
- *May:* Forty-one U-boats are sunk during the month. American and British convoys benefit from radar-equipped airplanes and from the British decoding of communication between U-boats. By month's end, the German pull many of their U-boats back from the North Atlantic. The U-boats are redeployed south and west of the Azores, where they pose a much smaller threat to Allied shipping.
- *May 9–14:* Some 238,000 German and Italian troops surrender in Tunisia to the Allied forces. The battle for North Africa is over.
- *June 19:* Propaganda minister Joseph Goebbels boasts that Berlin is now "free of Jews."
- *July 5:* German tank columns assail a bulge in the Russian line around the city of Kursk. Hitler has insisted upon this move, known as Operation Zitadelle, as a way to lure and then destroy the Russian armor.
- *July 9–10:* U.S. and British forces invade Sicily. They meet little resistance and much of the island is in Allied hands within a week. The entire island is taken on August 17.
- *July 12:* Russian tanks begin a major counterstrike to Operation Zitadelle. Over the next two days, Russian and German armor clash in what is probably the greatest tank battle in world history.
- *July 15:* Hitler calls off Operation Zitadelle. Known as the Battle of Kursk, it is a major victory for the Russians.
- *July 25:* Benito Mussolini is arrested by Italian police. On July 26, Marshal Pietro Badoglio takes control of the Italian government.

A soldier stops to rest at the memorial to the Italian soldier of World War I in Brolo, Sicily, August 1943. *(National Archives)*

- *August 3–10:* On two separate occasions, George Patton, commander of the U.S. Third Army, berates and slaps two U.S. soldiers in a military hospital on Sicily. Although not physically wounded, they suffer from battle fatigue, but Patton accuses them of cowardice. Attempts to hush up the incidents fail and there are calls for his dismissal. Eisenhower resists the pressure to replace Patton but forces Patton to make a public apology.
- *September 8:* Italy surrenders to the Allied Powers, ending its part in the war. The announcement catches the Germans by surprise, but they react swiftly.
- *September 10:* German forces enter Rome and place it under their control. Within the next 10 days, German units spread out through the Italian countryside, disarming Italian soldiers and replacing them with German soldiers.
- *September 12–13:* Benito Mussolini, under arrest since July 25, is held at a hotel in the Abruzzi Mountains. German SS soldiers come on gliders and rescue him from confinement. Mussolini is brought to

Germany, where he declares a new Italian state to be led from northern Italy.

- *October 13:* Led by Marshal Badoglio, Italy declares war on Germany.
- *November 5:* The Vatican is hit during Allied bombing of Rome.
- *November 6:* The Soviet army takes Kiev, the largest city of the Ukraine. The city and its people have been devastated by two years of occupation.
- *November 20:* U.S. Marines attack Tarawa Atoll in the Gilbert Islands. The marines find that the Japanese have dug in so deeply that most of them survived the fierce bombardment that preceded the landing.
- *November 23:* The struggle for Tarawa ends in a costly American victory.
- *November 28–December 1:* The first meeting between FDR, Churchill, and Stalin takes place in Tehran, the capital of Iran. The three men—soon known as the "Big Three"—concur that an Allied invasion of France will take place in 1944.
- *December 2:* Hitler calls on younger German boys to enlist. The age requirement will eventually be reduced to 15.
- *December 24:* FDR names Dwight Eisenhower to command Operation Overlord, the projected invasion of Europe. Chief of Staff George Marshall is disappointed, but his contributions to organizing the army's operations will be as crucial as any officer's in the war.
- *December 26:* The German battleship *Scharnhorst,* assigned to block an Allied convoy en route to Murmansk, Russia, is sunk; only 36 men survive of the crew of 1,900. From this date on, Allied convoys to the Russian coast meet little resistance.

1944

- *January–June:* A massive buildup of U.S. personnel and matériel takes place in southern England, in preparation for Operation Overlord. By the end of May, 3,000,000 Allied soldiers and 6,000,000 tons of supplies are gathered in England in preperation for Operation Overlord.
- *January 11:* The American P-51 Mustang makes its first appearance in dogfights over Germany. The 49 Mustangs that accompany bomber planes shoot down 15 German fighters and do not lose a single one of their own.

- *January 16:* Dwight Eisenhower arrives in London and takes up his duties as Supreme Commander of the Allied Expeditionary Force.
- *January 22:* U.S. and British forces land at Anzio and Nettuno, Italian coastal towns south of Rome. The daring landing is not followed up with speed, and the invaders bog down short of taking Rome.
- *January 27:* The siege of Leningrad ends after two and a half years. About 1 million inhabitants and 300,000 Russian soldiers have perished in the effort.
- *February 3:* U.S. ships shell areas of the Kurile Islands. This is the first time the U.S. Navy has reached the home islands of Japan.
- *February 15:* Allied bombers destroy the ancient abbey of Monte Cassino, halfway between Naples and Rome. The Germans quickly move into the rubble, and make Monte Cassino the linchpin of their defense of central Italy.
- *March 6:* The U.S. Air Force makes its first raid on Berlin. Six hundred sixty U.S. bombers are protected by 800 fighter planes.
- *March 18:* Hitler prepares his generals for what he knows will be an Allied invasion of France. Ever optimistic, Hitler declares, "Once defeated, the enemy will never try to invade again . . . an invasion failure would also deliver a crushing blow to the British and American morale."
- *April–May:* German leaders attempt to predict where the Allied blow will fall. Many of them are taken in by completely fictitious plans and preparations for invasion forces to land in the Calais area and Norway. Hitler, in a moment of intuition, predicts that the blow will fall in Normandy, but he does not follow up the insight with vigor. Field Marshal Rommel argues for mobile Panzer defense units that can strike as soon as the enemy lands. Rommel's plan is rendered useless by the fact that the best German Panzer units are far away, on the Russian front.
- *May 3:* Meat rationing ends in the United States.
- *May 17:* Polish troops enter the ruins of Monte Cassino, ending the long campaign for this strategic point.
- *June 4:* U.S. forces under Gen. Mark Clark liberate Rome, Italy.
- *June 4:* Eisenhower learns that the weather forecast for June 5, the day scheduled for the invasion, predicts conditions too dangerous for landing. Since many convoys are already at sea, however, he decides to proceed on June 6.

- *June 6:* D day: Operation Overlord begins. American, British, and Canadian soldiers land on five beaches in Normandy, France, surprising the German defenders. Once the initial shock has passed, the Germans put up a stiff resistance, fighting from pillboxes and other points. Thousands of Allied troops are killed, but the sheer weight of the attack brings the Allies ashore by early afternoon. The one serious opportunity the Germans have for a counterattack is thwarted by Hitler sleeping late that day; two SS Panzer units 15 miles back from the beaches cannot move without his permission. By the time Hitler awakes and gives the go-ahead, it is too late. Some 150,000 Allied troops are ashore by nightfall, and the Germans have lost their opportunity to win the battle on the beaches.
- *June 13:* Germans fire their first V-1 rockets at Britain. Six people are killed in London.
- *June 24:* FDR signs the Servicemen's Readjustment Act, which will later become known as the G.I. Bill of Rights.

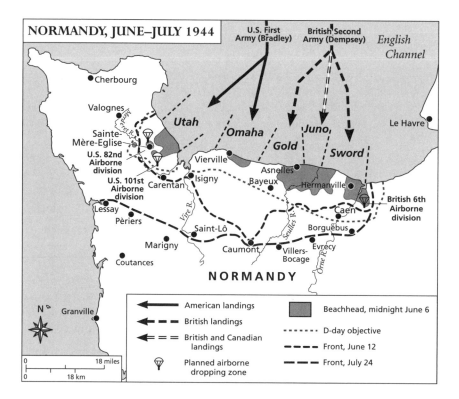

The bombs seen dropping toward this camouflaged Japanese plane destroyed it seconds after this photograph was taken. *(Library of Congress, Prints & Photographs Division [LC-USZ62-105392])*

- *July:* Intense fighting takes place in France, but the Allies gradually enlarge their holdings.
- *July 10:* The strategic city of Caen, Normandy, falls to the Allies.
- *July 16:* Rommel informs Berlin that the "unequal struggle" grows daily more insupportable. The next day he is wounded in an air attack and so he will return to his home in Germany.
- *July 20:* A number of prominent German civilians and military leaders have become convinced that Hitler must be disposed of so that Germany can negotiate with the Allies. Colonel Claus von Stauffenburg carries a bomb in his briefcase into a meeting with Hitler, then excuses himself. The explosion only wounds Hitler. Von Stauffenburg and his accomplices are rounded up and shot. Hitler becomes even more convinced in his destiny. In the weeks that follow, 7,000 people are arrested and 5,000 are executed.
- *July 30:* General Patton's Third Army breaks out of the Normandy region, heads south and east.

- *August 4:* Anne Frank, her parents, sister, and the four other people hiding in the annex in Amsterdam are arrested by the Germans. They are sent off to concentration camps, and only the father, Otto Frank, will survive. Returning to Amsterdam, he will be given a diary that Anne kept during their two years in hiding. It had been found and saved by a Dutch woman who had helped to hide the Franks. The diary will eventually become one of the best known books in the world.

- *August 7:* In Berlin, Hitler observes the rapid movement of Patton's Third Army, and believes he can trap the Americans. The Germans counterattack, hoping to take advantage of the extended Allied supply lines.

- *August 10:* American forces capture the island of Guam after 20 days of fighting.

- *August 10–20:* The Allies use the German counterattack to their advantage. The Germans suffer thousands of casualties, but due to a failure to "close the gap" at Falaise, many Germans escape the trap.

- *August 15:* Allied forces land in southern France between Cannes and Toulon. German resistance is weak because so many German troops are in the north, fighting the D day invasion.

- *August 25–26:* Allied forces, including the Free French, liberate Paris. Hitler had ordered the German commander to destroy the center of the city, but the commander had refused.

- *September 1:* Eisenhower sets up his headquarters in France and plans the final phase of the war. In an effort to show even-handedness, he allows British general Montgomery to play the leading role in Operation Market Garden.

- *September 17–25:* American and British paratroops undertake Operation Market Garden in the Netherlands. It is a costly failure.

- *October:* German resistance stiffens all along the line of the western front. Some Allied leaders had hoped the war would end by Christmas; this hope is now dashed.

- *October 14:* Hitler has come to suspect General Rommel of at least being sympathetic with the goal of those who attempted to assassinate him. Hitler's emissaries inform Rommel he is going to be put on trial unless takes the "honorable" way out. Rommel chooses to commit suicide rather than have his family dragged down in a trial. Though he had not participated in the plot to kill Hitler, Rommel's "defeatism" had cost him all support at the high command levels.

- *October 20:* U.S. forces land at Leyte Gulf in the Philippines. MacArthur delivers a radio address to the Filipinos: "People of the Philippines, I have returned!"
- *October 21:* American troops occupy Aachen, the first German city to fall into Allied hands.
- *October 23–26:* In the Leyte Gulf, U.S. and Japanese navies meet in the largest naval battle in human history. Although they enjoy some early success, the Japanese suffer the loss of four aircraft carriers, three battleships, six heavy cruisers, and 11 destroyers. Allied losses are comparatively light. The first kamikaze (suicide pilots) attack on a U.S. ship takes place on October 25.
- *October 24:* Hitler reveals his plan for a new offensive to two top generals. They are incredulous at first, but then begin to plan the campaign in great secrecy. The plan calls for a thrust through the

In England, members of the Special U.S. Naval Construction Battalion entertain their comrades, December 1944. Maintaining morale is serious business, and U.S. authorities attempted to suppress the spread of bad news such as the disastrous sinking of the U.S. troopship *Leopoldville* that same month. *(National Archives)*

Troops of the U.S. Seventh Armored Division advance along a road in Belgium during the Battle of the Bulge. *(Franklin D. Roosevelt Library)*

Ardennes Forest and the capture of Antwerp, Belgium, the major seaport for the unloading of Allied war matériel.

- *November 1:* FDR wins the presidential election for his fourth term. His new vice president is Harry Truman.
- *December:* Learning that the Russian army is on the nearby Vistula River, the Polish underground begins a massive revolt against the Germans in Warsaw. The Poles fight valiantly, expecting help from Russia. Instead, Stalin specifically forbids his tanks to move forward. By year's end, the Germans have completely suppressed the movement and killed many leading Poles.
- *December 16:* German units launch the first attack of the Battle of the Bulge in the Ardennes Forest. The weather—cold and rainy—favors the Germans, who achieve surprise and make surprising headway in the first 36 hours.
- *December 17–19:* The Germans continue to make progress. Most of the roads in the Ardennes sector funnel through the city of Bastogne, which Eisenhower is determined to hold at all costs. Units of the 101st U.S. Airborne, under General McAuliffe, hold the city.

- *December 22:* The Germans send a demand for surrender to the Bastogne garrison. General McAuliffe responds with a simple "Nuts!"—meaning the Germans could forget about that.
- *December 23:* The weather finally clears. Allied planes are able to hunt and destroy German tanks on the ground.
- *December 24:* The U.S. troopship *Leopoldville* is hit by a German plane and sinks in the English Channel. About 1,000 Americans perish in the ice-cold water. The disaster is large enough that U.S. intelligence keeps it secret for months.
- *December 26:* Patton's Third Army relieves the garrison at Bastogne. McAuliffe's men will ever afterward be known as the "Bastards of Bastogne."
- *December 30–January 27, 1945:* Allies conduct a counteroffensive against the Germans in the Ardennes and by January 27 will have regained all the territory given up.

1945

- *January 17:* The Soviet Army enters Warsaw, Poland.
- *February 4–11:* FDR, Churchill, and Stalin meet at Yalta, on the Black Sea coast. FDR is ailing, and he does not dominate the discussions as previously. Stalin gets Churchill and FDR to concede effective control over the countries of eastern Europe by promising to conduct free elections. Russia will also be allowed to conquer Berlin, regardless of whether Russian or American troops are closest to that city. Russia agrees to enter the war against Japan.
- *February 13–15:* British and U.S. pilots cooperate in the destruction of Dresden, Germany, from the air. Mainly due to a firestorm that results from the heavy bombing, more people are killed and buildings destroyed than the Germans had achieved in their 1940 blitz against London.
- *February 19–March 26:* U.S. forces capture the island of Iwo Jima at great cost both to the conquered and the conquerors.
- *March 7:* U.S. forces find a standing bridge over the Rhine at Remagen and the troops quickly rush across.
- *March 9:* Three hundred and thirty-four U.S. B-29 bombers pound Tokyo. The light, highly flammable Japanese buildings explode in flame. Between 80,000 and 100,000 Japanese die on this one night.

- *March 17:* The bridge at Remagen collapses from the heavy use it has experienced in the last 10 days. By now, the Americans have constructed numerous pontoon bridges across the river.
- *April 1–June 22:* The Battle of Okinawa rages on that small Pacific island. The Japanese are well dug in and most of them fight to the last.
- *April 6:* The Japanese naval command sends virtually all its remaining ships in a suicidal attack on the American fleet off Okinawa. The Japanese flagship is the super-battleship *Yamamoto,* pride of the Japanese fleet.
- *April 7:* In the Battle of the East China Sea, the *Yamamoto* and most of its attendant vessels are sunk by relentless air attacks from U.S. planes.
- *April 11:* U.S. troops liberate the concentration camp at Buchenwald.
- *April 12:* FDR dies at Warm Springs, Georgia, from a cerebral hemorrhage. Condolences pour in from around the world. Harry Truman is sworn in as the new president. Almost at once, Truman learns that scientists in New Mexico are close to being ready to detonate an atom bomb.
- *April 12:* Eisenhower visits the liberated concentration camp at Ohrdurf. Horrified by what he sees—emaciated human beings and actual skeletons—Eisenhower orders that all U.S. troops in the vicinity visit the death camp.
- *April 13:* The Soviet Army enters Vienna.
- *April 19:* U.S. troops liberate the concentration camp at Dachau.
- *April 25:* The representatives of 50 nations meet in San Francisco. They begin to draw up a document that will establish the United Nations Organization.
- *April 25:* U.S. and Russian soldiers meet on the Elbe River. Despite the language barrier, the two groups get on well. They have broken the German Reich in two, and the end is near at hand.
- *April 25:* The final battle for Berlin begins. While the last German units fight heroic battles against the mass of Russians, Hitler becomes increasingly delusional in his bunker. Just two weeks earlier, he had rejoiced to learn of FDR's death and nourished hopes that the war would turn in his favor.
- *April 30:* Hitler and his wife of one day, Eva Braun, commit suicide in the bunker; their bodies are cremated. Russian troops reach Hitler's bunker and fly their flag over the Reichstag, Germany's parliament building.

(*Top*) German officers sign unconditional surrender in Reims, France, May 7, 1945, and (*bottom*) Allied leaders at the signing. *(Franklin D. Roosevelt Library)*

- *May 2:* The remnants of the German army in Italy surrender.
- *May 7:* The Germans sign a surrender document at General Eisenhower's headquarters in France. Military operations are to end on May 8, which will be celebrated as Victory in Europe (V-E) Day by all

the Allied peoples. Some German units engage in minor hostilities for the next week.

- *July 16:* American scientists watch the detonation of a nuclear bomb in the desert of New Mexico.
- *July 17–August 2:* Truman meets with Prime Minister Clement Atlee (who has replaced Churchill) and Stalin at Potsdam, Germany. On the first day, Truman is informed by code of the successful nuclear detonation; he will inform only Churchill. A broadcast from Potsdam on July 26 calls on Japan to surrender unconditionally; because this so-called Potsdam Declaration does not say anything about what will be done with the Japanese emperor, it is sometimes blamed for stiffening Japanese resistance and thus justifying the use of the atomic bomb.
- *July 28:* The Senate consents to the United Nations Charter by a vote of 89-2.
- *August 6:* A U.S. bomber, the *Enola Gay,* drops an atomic bomb on Hiroshima. At least 100,000 Japanese are killed outright, and many others are wounded.
- *August 8:* Russia declares war on Japan.
- *August 9:* Another U.S. bomber drops a second atomic bomb, this one on Nagasaki. The death toll is at least 70,000. Both Hiroshima and Nagasaki suffer massive destruction.
- *August 10:* The Japanese government agrees to surrender. It asks only that Emperor Hirohito be allowed to remain in his position.
- *August 12:* Soviet Russia enters the war against Japan. Russian tanks cross the border into Manchuria and make significant gains.
- *August 15:* Emperor Hirohito goes on the radio and explains to his people they have lost the war. For most of the Japanese, this is the first time they have heard his voice. For the Allies, this is V-J Day. It will be several weeks before all of Japan's military units around the Pacific surrender.
- *September 2:* Surrender ceremonies are conducted aboard the USS *Missouri,* where MacArthur treats the Japanese officials with dignity. Only later do Allied leaders learn that a large group of kamikaze pilots had lined up at Tokyo that day, preparing to attack the ceremony in progress. They were dissuaded by the arrival of the Japanese crown prince.

Results

World War II was by far the most devastating and costly of all wars known to humankind. Most observers agree that about 10,000,000 Russian military personnel were killed, wounded, or missing. Germany lost perhaps 4,000,000. The United States lost some 410,000 military. Great Britain had some 270,000 military deaths, with another 90,000 civilian deaths. Six million Jews were rounded up and killed by the Germans (as were some 250,000 Romanies [formerly known as Gypsies]). The numbers of other noncombatants lost is almost incalculable—a conservative estimate would be some 20,000,000, almost half of whom were Chinese, while the USSR claims close to this number. Putting a price tag on the war is even more elusive, especially if indirect yet real costs—such as medical bills and veteran pensions—are to be included.

In geopolitical terms, the results of the war were far-reaching. The war spelled the end for colonial empires everywhere. Britain left India in 1947, and France was forced out of Indochina in 1954. Indigenous peoples around the world demanded, and received, nations of their own with votes in the UN General Assembly. The war ended with much of Europe in ruins and with world power almost equally divided between the United States and the USSR (Soviet Union). That division of power led to the cold war, which lasted until about 1991.

The war also brought forth new weapons and technologies that would play important roles in the future—the aircraft carrier and radar, to single out just one of each. Above all, the invention of nuclear weapons, and their use against Japan, created the atomic era. Every person on Earth since August 1945 entered a world changed by World War II.

9

THE KOREAN WAR

Korea was free and independent until 1910, when it was annexed by Japan. The Japanese held Korea, exploiting its work force and raw materials, until the last weeks of World War II. On August 8, 1945, as the war in the Pacific was about to end, the Soviet Union invaded Korea from the north. U.S. troops entered the southern part of the peninsula, and the Russians and Americans made a rough division of the peninsula at the 38th parallel. Even though Russian and American soldiers left by 1949, no agreement could be reached between the two areas that had been occupied. The northern area, dominated by Korean Communists, became the Democratic People's Republic of Korea and the southern part, dominated by Koreans who favored a capitalist economy, became the Republic of Korea.

In a secret visit with Stalin in fall 1949 (only revealed many years later by Nikita Khrushchev) Kim Il Sung, the Communist leader of North Korea, informs Stalin of his plan to invade South Korea, and Stalin does not try to dissuade him. During the winter of 1949–50, North Korean leaders looked to both Soviet Russia and Communist China for military aid. U.S. policy makers were unaware of Kim's intention, and the American people as a whole were unaware of the situation. That changed in summer 1950.

1950

- *January 12:* Secretary of State Dean Acheson, speaking to the National Press Club in Washington, delineates the perimeters around

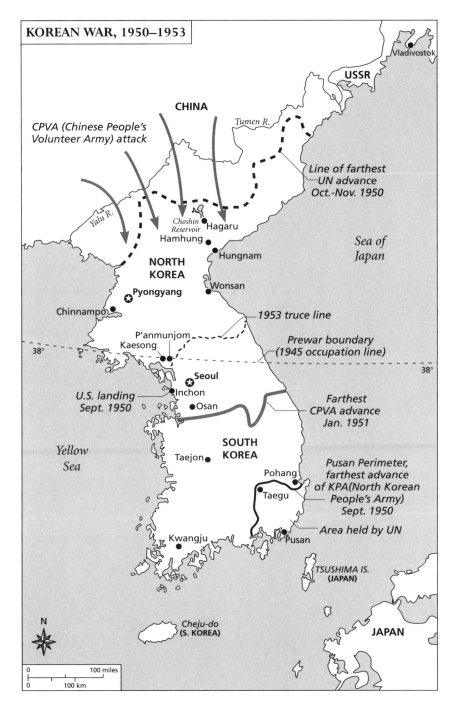

KOREAN WAR, 1950–1953

Vladivostok

USSR

CHINA

Tumen R.

CPVA (Chinese People's
Volunteer Army) attack

Line of farthest
UN advance
Oct.-Nov. 1950

Yalu R.

Choshin
Reservoir
Hagaru

Hamhung

Hungnam

NORTH
KOREA

Sea of
Japan

Pyongyang

Wonsan

Chinnampo

1953 truce line

P'anmunjom
Kaesong

Prewar boundary
(1945 occupation line)

38°

38°

Seoul

U.S. landing
Sept. 1950

Inchon

Osan

Farthest
CPVA advance
Jan. 1951

Yellow
Sea

SOUTH
KOREA

Taejon

Pohang

Pusan Perimeter,
farthest advance
of KPA(North Korean
People's Army)
Sept. 1950

Taegu

Area held by UN

Kwangju

Pusan

TSUSHIMA IS.
(JAPAN)

N

Cheju-do
(S. KOREA)

JAPAN

0   100 miles
0   100 km

East Asia that the United States will defend. Acheson does not include South Korea.

- *March:* North Korea receives military aid from the Soviet Union, tanks in particular. But Stalin pulls the remaining Soviet military advisers out of North Korea and also sends a message: "If you should get kicked in the teeth, I shall not lift a finger." Stalin is willing to help destabilize the region, but his greater attention is on western Europe.
- *May 13–16:* Kim Il Sung, the leader of North Korea, visits Mao Zedong (Mao Tse-tung) in Beijing (Peking). Mao attempts to discourage Kim from making an attack on South Korea.
- *June 17:* American diplomat and foreign-policy expert John Foster Dulles visits the South Korean military station at the 38th parallel. Although North Korea has massed troops and tanks just a few miles beyond, Dulles and his aides see no sign of the buildup.
- *June 25:* In the predawn hours, North Korea launches an intense artillery barrage and then invades South Korea. The North Koreans achieve a complete surprise. They break through the line along the 38th parallel and head south.

A soldier bids his wife and son goodbye as he leaves for Korea in 1950. *(National Archives)*

President Harry Truman is in Independence, Missouri, when he is informed of the invasion. His first response is "By God, I'm going to let them have it." Later this afternoon, in New York City, the United Nations Security Council, after condemning the attack by North Korea, votes 9-0 (the USSR is boycotting the Security Council and so is not present; Yugoslavia abstains) to demand that North Korea withdraw from the areas it has already seized.

Truman immediately authorizes U.S. planes and bombers based in Japan to commence attacks on the North Korean invaders.

- *June 26:* In Washington, Truman orders the U.S. Seventh Fleet into the Formosa Strait, the waters between Formosa and mainland China.
- *June 27:* In New York, the UN Security Council votes "to furnish such assistance . . . as may be necessary" to South Korea. It will be this decision, not any formal declaration of war by the U.S. Congress, that allows President Truman to commit U.S. forces to fighting in Korea.
- *June 28:* U.S. planes and bombers go into action over Korea. Seoul, the capital of South Korea, has fallen to the North Koreans on this day.
- *June 29:* General MacArthur and seven high-ranking U.S. officers fly from Japan to South Korea. They observe the fighting and conclude that "The South Korean forces are in confusion, have not seriously fought, and lack leadership." In Washington, Truman authorizes U.S. naval and air strikes north of the 38th parallel.
- *June 30:* In Japan, MacArthur puts together Task Force Smith, named for its commander, Lt. Col. Charles Smith. Composed of just 500 men, who have been on peacetime duty in Japan, this is all that is available to throw into the action in South Korea.
- *July 5:* Task Force Smith is the first to meet North Koreans in combat. The U.S. troops withdraw, and the withdrawal becomes a rout. Marguerite Higgins, an American journalist, reports seeing fellow Americans "throw down their arms, cursing their government for what they thought was embroilment in a hopeless cause." This and other reports only serve to stiffen the American resolve to act in Korea.
- *July 7:* The United Nations votes to create an international task force to defend South Korea. In deference to the significant contribution made by the U.S., President Truman is allowed to name the overall commander for the UN soldiers.
- *July 8:* General MacArthur is named commander of the UN forces in North Korea. Leader of the U.S. Pacific forces during World War II,

MacArthur has been leader of the U.S. military occupation of Japan since 1945.

- *July 14–15:* North Korean troops cross the Kum River. The loss of this natural defense is a major setback for the defenders.
- *July 19–20:* Gen. William Dean, commander of U.S. forces in the field, decides to try to hold the line at Taejon. But after two days of intense fighting the Americans are forced to evacuate. General Dean escapes at the last minute in a jeep but is forced to abandon it and take to the hills. Five weeks later he will be captured, and he is held as a prisoner of war until the very end.
- *July 29:* Gen. Walton Walker, commander of the U.S. Eighth Army, issues a "stand or die" order to his men. Any further retreat, he says, would lead to enormous butchery and failure.
- *August 2:* By this date all of South Korea except the small enclave around the southern port city of Pusan has fallen to North Korea. U.S. forces hold the 5,000-square-mile area, the so-called Pusan Perimeter. General Walker deploys his limited forces in tactical maneuvers that enable him to maintain the position.
- *August 31:* The North Koreans launch their last major attack on the Pusan Perimeter. They are pushed back by September 5: The American line has held. By now, too, the North Korean army had suffered extremely heavy losses in troops, tanks, and other matériel.
- *September 15:* General MacArthur launches Operation Chromite. One of the most daring amphibious operations in military history, Chromite involves U.S. troops landing at the port city of Inchon, on the Yellow Sea. It is 180 miles northwest of the Pusan Perimeter and so far behind most of the North Korean army. Inchon is known for the height of its tides, making it seem a most unlikely place for the UN forces to land. The element of surprise is attained, and MacArthur's troops meet little resistance.
- *September 16–19:* Some 55,000 Americans disembark at Inchon, having completed one of the boldest initiatives seen in modern warfare. In so doing, they are in a position to cut off the North Korean forces to the south, but MacArthur chooses not to send his forces across to the eastern coast, and this leaves a corridor for the North Koreans to retreat.
- *September 16–19:* General Walker's troops make offensives all along the line of the Pusan Perimeter. After three days of fighting, the North Koreans begin to retreat.

Korean women and children search the rubble of Seoul for anything that can be used or burned as fuel. Although the U.S. presence returned Seoul to the control of Syngman Rhee, the North Korean attack left the city devastated. *(National Archives)*

- *September 25–28:* Fighting rages in and around Seoul. The North Koreans fight with wild despair, using barricades and houses as pillboxes. It takes four days of street fighting to complete the reconquest.
- *September 26:* U.S. B-29 bombers strike one of North Korea's largest hydroelectric plants.
- *September 29:* MacArthur officially turns over Seoul to Syngman Rhee, president of the Republic of Korea (ROK). Both MacArthur and Rhee weep during the proceedings. During this day, too, South Korean soldiers reach the 38th parallel. Although there are still some small units of North Koreans in South Korea, the situation is now pretty much restored to where it was before June 25.
- *September 30:* Zhou Enlai (Chou-En-lai), the Chinese foreign minister, warns in a speech that "The Chinese people enthusiastically love peace, but [will not] tolerate seeing their neighbors being savagely invaded by the imperialists." Within two weeks, thousands of Chinese troops will begin moving secretly into North Korea.

CHRONOLOGY OF WARS

- *October 1–10:* Now determined to take over North Korea, President Syngman Rhee has ordered his forces to proceed north of the 38th parallel. They meet little resistance, and by October 10 have reached the major port of Wonsan.
- *October 9:* U.S. soldiers cross the 38th parallel. They have now joined the Republic of Korea forces in a full-scale invasion of North Korea.
- *October 15:* President Truman and General MacArthur meet in person on Wake Island. It is their first meeting. Truman expresses concerns about the possibility of a wider conflict; MacArthur appears supremely confident. While they appear relaxed, even jaunty for the photographers, both men come away with deeper suspicions about the other. Truman's vision of MacArthur as a grandstander is confirmed. MacArthur's belief that the president is "soft" on communism continues.
- *October 16–24:* Soldiers of the People's Republic of China cross the Yalu River and take up positions in North Korea. These men—many of them veterans of the long Chinese Civil War between the Nationalists and the Communists—use camouflage effectively, and their approach is concealed.
- *October 20–22:* UN forces capture Pyongyang, the capital of North Korea. This is the high point of the U.S. counteroffensive, which has resulted in greater success than anyone—except perhaps Mac-Arthur—had hoped.
- *October 26:* Some units of the South Korean army reach the Yalu River, the border between North Korea and China. This same day sees the first clash between Chinese troops and UN forces—actually, a South Korean unit—about 40 miles south of the Yalu River. MacArthur refuses to believe that the Chinese are present in any great numbers.
- *November 1:* The first clash between Chinese troops and U.S. forces occurs at the town of Unsan. This same day, another unit of U.S. troops gets to within 18 miles of the Yalu River, the closest U.S. forces get to the border with China.
- *November 2:* U.S. Marines hold off the Chinese attackers near Unsan but in general the U.S. forces are beaten back by the Chinese.
- *November 7:* After several days of attacking the South Korean and U.S. forces, the Chinese pull back into the mountains.
- *November 8:* In the first aerial dogfight between jet planes in the history of warfare, U.S. Air Force F-80s shoot down one Chinese MiG.

- *November 8–18:* Without clearance from Washington, MacArthur authorizes 10 days of bombing raids on the bridges over the Yalu River and many North Korean cities and facilities. Because they appear to be effective, Washington allows MacArthur to proceed.
- *November 23:* U.S. troops celebrate Thanksgiving Day in North Korea. Optimism is high; most of the U.S. military expect to drive the Chinese attackers out and be home for Christmas.
- *November 24:* MacArthur makes an aerial reconnaissance of the Yalu River. He sees no sign of the camouflaged Chinese. UN forces go on the offensive again.
- *November 25:* The U.S. Eighth Army is caught completely off guard by "human wave attacks" by the Chinese. Heedless of the cost of human life, the Chinese hurl themselves at the American positions and make considerable headway. Even U.S. veterans of World War II cannot remember fighting an enemy so ruthless and determined.
- *November 26–27:* Chinese soldiers make massive attacks all along the line against UN defenders. The weather turns bitterly cold, an event for which the Chinese are better prepared than the Americans.
- *November 27–December 11:* U.S. Marines are caught by the Chinese in the hills around the Chosin Reservoir. With the temperature around zero and short of food and supplies, the men undertake a harrowing retreat. Before they finally arrive at the port city of Hungnam, the U.S. forces have suffered 4,500 killed, wounded, or captured.
- *November 28:* MacArthur cables the Pentagon: "We face an entirely new war."
- *December:* Truman issues an order that requires that all official statements about the war, whether made by leaders in Washington or abroad, must be cleared through official channels. It is clearly a "gag order," aimed at MacArthur.
- *December 5:* UN forces abandon Pyongyang, North Korea's capital.
- *December 8:* Truman announces a ban on all shipments of goods from the United States to China.
- *December 16:* Confronted by the drastic series of defeats since the Chinese entered the war, Truman declares a national emergency.
- *December 17–24:* The U.S. evacuates some 22,000 of its forces from the port of Hungnam; 80,000 other UN troops and 90,000 Korean refugees are also evacuated.

- *December 23:* Gen. Walton Walker, commander of the U.S. forces in Korea, is killed when his jeep swerves into a ditch to avoid a major collision.
- *December 26:* Gen. Matthew Ridgway arrives in North Korea as the new commander of the Eighth Army. He is under MacArthur's command, but MacArthur gives Ridgway full discretion as to matters on the ground.
- *December 31:* The Chinese launch a new "Third Phase Offensive."

1951

- *January 4:* UN forces abandon Seoul.
- *January 5:* Inchon, the site of MacArthur's 1950 landing, is abandoned by UN troops. Within days the U.S. line has fallen below the 38th parallel. The 285-mile retreat, from U.S. positions when the Chinese first attacked on November 1, is the longest in U.S. military history.
- *January 25:* Ridgway starts Operation Thunderbolt. The U.S. Eighth Army and South Korean forces advance north.
- *February 1–8:* At the Kuje-do Island camp where increasing numbers of North Koreans are held as prisoners of war, a feared riot leads to machine gun fire and the death of two prisoners. This is only the beginning of mounting unrest among the POWs.
- *February 11–17:* The Chinese Fourth Phase Offensive is launched. The major Chinese effort comes in the area held by the U.S. Second Division.
- *February 13–15:* Fighting rages for control of an area near Chipyong-ni, known as the Battle of the Twin Tunnels after the railroad tunnels in the area. The U.S. Fifth Cavalry breaks through and relieves the UN positions on February 15.
- *March 14:* MacArthur sends a message to the Chinese leaders, threatening all-out war if China does not withdraw from Korea. He ridicules their bombing capacity and predicts that he will soon bring them to the point of collapse.
- *March 15:* In the face of advancing UN forces, the Chinese abandon Seoul, the fourth time the city has changed hands in the course of the war.
- *March 15:* In a violation of Truman's gag order, MacArthur tells the Associated Press that stopping the UN Army at the 38th parallel was contrary to the goal of unifying Korea.

Members of the First Marine Division capture Chinese Communists during fighting on the central Korean front, March 2, 1951.
(National Archives)

- *March–April:* The Chinese are massing their soldiers in the so-called Iron Triangle, a plateau surrounded by mountains, north of the 38th parallel, in central Korea.
- *April 5:* Republican congressman Joseph Martin releases a letter that MacArthur has recently sent to him. In the letter, MacArthur concurs with Martin that Nationalist Chinese troops should be called in to fight and, in an obvious dig at Truman, states that "In war there is no substitute for victory."
- *April 5–21:* U.S. forces conduct Operation Rugged and achieve considerable success in pushing the Chinese back.
- *April 11:* After sounding out the opinion of all his top advisers as to how he should best handle MacArthur, Truman dismisses him from all his command positions. Critics assail the president, but Truman remains tough. When General Eisenhower receives the news and is asked to comment, he replies, "I am going to remain silent in every language known to man." Few Americans know that Eisenhower and MacArthur—who appear friendly in public—have little liking for one another.

- *April 12:* General Ridgway replaces MacArthur as the UN commander of forces in Korea.
- *April 19:* General MacArthur addresses a joint session of Congress. MacArthur urges the nation's representatives to expand to the war against Communist China. He concludes the speech with an emotional farewell: "Old soldiers never die, they just fade away." Despite a powerful swell of support for the fired general, MacArthur will never again be a force in American public life.
- *April 22–30:* The Chinese conduct their spring offensive along a 40-mile front. Although the UN forces retreat to some degree, they do not give up Seoul.
- *April 23–26:* Four thousand British soldiers of the Twenty-ninth Brigade resist overwhelming Chinese attacks. Some 850 men of the Gloucestershire Regiment are cut off from the rest; only 169 of them make it back to the main British lines.
- *May:* The Chinese offensive peters out. Entire Chinese units surrender in some circumstances. Their American captors are amazed at the primitive state of equipment and supplies that many of the Chinese are fighting with.

U.S. Air Force B-26 (Invader) light bombers release quarter-ton demolition bombs in a strike over North Korea and Chinese Communist forces, October 1951. *(National Archives)*

- *May 9:* U.S. planes bomb North Korea's temporary capital, Sinuiju, the largest air raid of the war.
- *June 1–24:* UN forces commence another offensive and drive the Chinese farther north. But it is now clear to both sides that they face a stalemate—or more and more casualties—if one or another side continues to go on the offensive.
- *June 23:* Jacob Malik, the Soviet ambassador to the United Nations, proposes a cease-fire in Korea. China's official newspaper will endorse this two days later.
- *June 30:* Ridgway announces that the UN is ready to discuss an armistice.
- *July 1:* The North Koreans agree to armistice talks.
- *July 10:* Talks commence between North Korea and the UN at the South Korean city of Kaesong.
- *August 18–October 15:* UN forces go on the attack in the hilly region known as Punchbowl. In hard-fought battles they eventually take Bloody Ridge and then Heartbreak Ridge. Casualties on both sides are extremely heavy.
- *October 24:* In daylight bombing raid, four U.S. B-29s are shot down by Chinese MiGs and three others are seriously damaged. This will put an end to daylight bombing raids.
- *October 25:* Truce talks resume.
- *November 27–December 21:* In what is known as the "Little Armistice," both sides agree to regard their present positions as the demarcation line until a permanent agreement is reached.

1952

- *January:* UN artillery and air attacks are made against Communist positions. The offensive lasts all month.
- *January–May:* Discontent builds at the POW camps in South Korea.
- *January 7:* Dwight Eisenhower makes public his willingness to be drafted for the Republican Party presidential nomination.
- *March–August:* U.S. plans to conduct massive bombing raids on North Korean targets. By the end, North Korea has lost almost all of its electrical power capacity and its capital, Pyongyang, is leveled.
- *May 7–11:* Gen. Frank Dodd, commander of the Kuje-do POW camp, is seized and held hostage by prisoners. He is released, but only

after the officer assigned to negotiate with the POWs agrees to their terms. Both officers will be reduced in rank.

- *May 12:* Ridgway leaves to become supreme NATO commander, replacing General Eisenhower. Gen. Matthew Clark replaces Ridgway in Korea.
- *June 6–September 21:* UN troops carry out Operation Counter to occupy a line of hills in west-central Korea. Among the bloodiest battles that take place during this period are those for Pork Chop Hill and Old Baldy Hill. Even after the UN forces finally capture these hills, fighting will continue sporadically until the Chinese launch a major attack in March 1953.
- *June 10:* The new commander of the Kuje-do POW camp orders an attack to impose order on the camp; before it is over, 31 POWs and one U.S. soldier are dead, and more than 150 men are wounded.
- *October:* Dwight Eisenhower makes a pledge on television that he will go to Korea to observe the situation firsthand if he is elected president.
- *November 4:* Dwight Eisenhower and Richard Nixon win election as president and vice president. They are the first Republican ticket to win a presidential election since Herbert Hoover in 1928.
- *December:* An attempt by POWs to break out at Pongam-do is suppressed.
- *December 4–5:* Eisenhower visits North Korea.

1953

- *January 20:* Dwight Eisenhower is inaugurated.
- *March 5:* Joseph Stalin, premier and leader of the Soviet Union since 1927, dies in Moscow. His death brings to an end the most ruthlessly expansionistic era in Soviet history.
- *March 23–July 11:* The Chinese carry out assaults on Old Baldy Hill and Pork Chop Hill. They take Old Baldy by March 26, but the United States holds out on Pork Chop Hill for week after week until finally abandoning it.
- *March 28:* North Korea indicates a willingness to exchange sick and wounded prisoners of war.
- *June 10–30:* A Chinese offensive takes two outpost positions and pushes the South Korean army back to a new "Main Line of Resistance," about three miles further south.
- *July 10:* Negotiators reach agreement on all major points.

Gen. W. K. Harrison, Jr. (left), and Gen. Nam Il (right) sign armistice documents, July 23, 1953. *(National Archives)*

- *July 13:* The final Chinese offensive begins. Although the UN forces halt the Chinese after a week, both sides take heavy casualties and it is clear that the Chinese are still prepared to fight.
- *July 27:* An armistice is signed, ending the war. North and South Korea are divided at the 38th parallel, almost exactly where they had been when the war began, three years and one month earlier.

Results

The war ends with the boundary between North and South Korea at roughly the 38th parallel. Neither side has gained in territory or strategic advantage. The human losses are staggering for such a limited war. About 1 million North and South Korean soldiers and some 2 million Korean civilians have been killed; another 2 million have been wounded or become displaced persons. Estimates of Chinese losses run from between 200,000 to 1 million dead. U.S. casualties are 54,246 dead, of whom 20,617 died of wounds, in accidents, or from other war-related causes; more than 12,000 are missing in action and presumed dead. UN forces (other than South Koreans) count some 3,000 dead, 12,000 wounded, and 2,000 missing in action (and presumed dead). No dollar values have ever been assigned to the material losses of any of the participants; the destruction of both South and North Korean property was incalculable. The United States alone spent close to $100 billion (in 2002 dollars); other UN nations spent about $25 billion.

No country truly benefited from the war. North and South Korea developed a permanent distrust, even a hatred for one another. Communist China made no gains during the war and even lost face because of its failure to overrun the UN forces. The United States suffered some early humiliations and then learned some significant military lessons, but the casualty count casts doubt on their value. Perhaps only the United Nations made some gain: For the first time in human history an international body, bent on peace between nations, acted in order to prevent the takeover of one country by another.

10

THE VIETNAM WAR

In 1883, Vietnam submitted to French colonial rule. After World War I, Nguyen Ai Quoc—who will later adopt the name Ho Chi Minh—asked the Versailles Peace Conference members to support Vietnamese independence. Ignored by Western powers, he will later emerge as modern Vietnam's greatest leader, despite French installation of Bao Dai as emperor.

1940–1954

- In 1940 France's Vichy government yields Vietnam to Japan. In 1941, Ho Chi Minh returns to Vietnam, and the Vietnam Independence League, or Vietminh, begins its freedom struggle, now aimed at the Japanese. The United States provides funds to this resistance movement and the U.S. Office of Strategic Service (OSS) sends in trainers. At World War II's end, Ho Chi Minh announces formation of the Democratic Republic of Vietnam, but the French reoccupy Vietnam and by February 1946 the French are fighting the Vietminh. (The first U.S. serviceman's death occurred in September 1945 when OSS officer Peter Dewey was shot by Vietminh forces.) The United States recognizes the French-propped Bao Dai government, but the Vietminh continues to resist, defeating the French at Dien Bien Phu after an epic siege (March 13 to May 7, 1954). At peace talks in Geneva, all parties agree to a temporary division of Vietnam along the 17th parallel (July 20–21, 1954). Ho Chi Minh and his Vietminh proclaim North Vietnam to be the Democratic Republic of Vietnam on October 11, 1954. By this time, the United States already has some 350 members of the

Military Assistance Advisory Group (MAAG) helping the South Vietnamese in various capacities.

1955–1960

- In South Vietnam, U.S.-backed Ngo Dinh Diem proclaims himself president of the Republic of Vietnam (October 26, 1955). Ho Chi Minh begins to organize increasingly more active guerrilla and terrorist operations in an effort to overthrow the South Vietnam government. On October 22, 1957, 13 Americans are wounded in bombings of offices of the MAAG and the U.S. Information Service in Saigon. On July 8, 1959, two U.S. servicemen with MAAG are killed during a guerrilla attack outside Saigon. In December 1960, the North Vietnamese announce the formation of the National Front for the Liberation of the South; the South Vietnamese will call their members the Vietcong, a contraction designed to tag them as "Communist Vietnamese."

1961

- *January:* By John F. Kennedy's inauguration, the United States has 900 military advisers in Vietnam. Kennedy follows a counterinsurgency policy, increasing advisers. In the ensuing months, they will become increasingly more involved in combat operations.
- *December 31:* The United States now has some 3,200 military personnel in Vietnam. They are authorized to fire back when fired on. U.S. Navy ships are offshore and planes are flying missions from aircraft carriers. Fourteen Americans have been killed.

1962

- *January 13:* Operation Ranch Hand commences its project of defoliating parts of South Vietnam to expose the Vietcong's movements. The main chemical used is known as Agent Orange (2,4,5-T), named after the color of its metal containers.
- *January 15:* At a press conference, President Kennedy refers to the situation in Vietnam and uses the phrase "light at the end of the tunnel." In the years that follow, other leaders will repeat this phrase, but it will soon become repeated with increasingly bitter irony by those opposed to the war.
- *February 4:* The first U.S. helicopter is shot down.

- *February 8:* Gen. Paul D. Harkins is installed in Saigon as commander of all U.S. military operations. In the months that follow, U.S. military personnel will take increasingly active roles.
- *December 31:* Some 11,000 U.S. advisory and support personnel are now in Vietnam; in 1962, 109 Americans have been wounded or killed.

1963

- *January 2:* In the Mekong Delta, a highly equipped force of 2,500 South Vietnamese troops (ARVN) fails to defeat a group of only some 300 Vietcong. U.S. advisers realize that the South Vietnamese are going to need a lot of help.
- *May 8:* Eleven civilians, mostly Buddhists, die during a demonstration in the old colonial capital city of Hue. The Buddhists become more active in protesting the regime of President Diem; particularly hated are the secret police headed by his younger brother, Ngo Dinh Nhu.
- *June 11:* A 73-year-old Buddhist monk, Thich Quang Duc, immolates himself publicly to protest the government's mistreatment of Buddhists. More such immolations follow in the ensuing weeks. Madame Nhu, wife of President Diem's brother, dismisses these incidents as "barbecues." Her remark reinforces her nickname, "the Dragon Lady."
- *November 1–2:* Duong Van ("Big") Minh leads a coup against President Diem. After surrendering on November 2, Diem and his brother Nhu are assassinated. Although the U.S. government does not appear to have promoted such an action, its representatives in Vietnam did not do everything they might have to stop it. Only years later will the public learn the full story of the actions of certain U.S. officials.
- *November 22:* President Kennedy is assassinated. By this time he had increased the number of U.S. military personnel in Vietnam to 16,500; 76 Americans have died. Vice President Lyndon B. Johnson assumes the presidency and announces that he intends to continue Kennedy's policies in Vietnam.

1964

- *January 2:* President Johnson receives a report known as Oplan 34A, prepared by civilian and military members of the Defense

Department. It outlines an ambitious commitment of the U.S. military to attack North Vietnam.

- *January 17:* Five American helicopter crewmen die when ARVN troops attack insurgents in the Mekong Delta.
- *January 27:* Secretary of Defense Robert McNamara tells a congressional committee that the "bulk of the U.S. armed forces in Vietnam can be expected to leave by the end of 1965."
- *January 30:* Maj. Gen. Nguyen Khanh leads a coup and takes over the government of South Vietnam.
- *June 20:* At the U.S. Military Assistance Command Vietnam (MACV) Gen. William Westmoreland becomes commander of U.S. forces in Vietnam.
- *July 6:* The Vietcong attack the Nam Dong Special Forces camp, killing two U.S. soldiers. Cap. Roger H. C. Donlon wins the first Medal of Honor awarded for service in Vietnam.
- *July 11–12:* ARVN forces lose 200 during an attack on their Chuong Thien post.
- *July 30:* U.S. destroyer *Maddox* enters the Gulf of Tonkin on a spying assignment. South Vietnamese raid the nearby North Vietnamese islands of Hon Me and Hon Ngu.
- *August 2:* Three North Vietnamese patrol boats fire torpedoes at the *Maddox,* but the *Maddox* sinks one of the patrol boats and disables the others.
- *August 4:* In the night, the *Maddox* believes it is being attacked again by enemy torpedo boats and calls in air support from a carrier. Neither the ship's crew nor the pilots actually see any boats and the *Maddox's* captain soon reports that there probably was no attack. But reports of the incident are immediately relayed to Washington officials.
- *August 5:* On orders from Washington, the carriers *Ticonderoga* and *Constellation* launch planes for 64 attacks against North Vietnam. Two U.S. planes are hit and one pilot is killed. Lt. Everett Alvarez is shot down and becomes the first U.S. pilot held by the North Vietnamese.
- *August 7:* Congress passes what becomes known as the Tonkin Gulf Resolution, authorizing President Johnson to take appropriate steps in response to North Vietnamese actions. This is the closest the U.S. government comes to a declaration of war against North Vietnam.
- *October 30:* Vietcong shelling of Bien Hoa air base kills five U.S. soldiers.

- *November 3:* President Johnson is reelected by a landslide.
- *December:* In secret White House meetings, Johnson approves air campaigns against North Vietnam if provoked. Secret air strikes in Laos begin.
- *December 31:* U.S. advisers number 23,300; American casualties during 1964 are 147 dead, 11 missing, 1,138 injured.

1965

- *January 2:* Five Americans are killed and three wounded at Binh Gia, the highest casualties in a single battle up to now.
- *February 6–7:* Camp Holloway, the major U.S. Army installation, undergoes attack. Vietcong ground and mortar fire kill eight U.S. soldiers. In Operation Flaming Dart, 49 aircraft from U.S. carriers bomb North Vietnam's Dong Hai for three days, beginning the air war against North Vietnam.
- *February 10:* Twenty-three Americans are killed at Qui Nhon by Vietcong shells, the most in one attack so far. Operation Flaming Dart II becomes the biggest air offensive against North Vietnam so far.
- *March 2:* Operation Rolling Thunder, a bombing initiative against North Vietnam, begins.

Napalm bombs explode on Viet Cong structures south of Saigon in 1965.
(National Archives)

- *March 8–12:* Some 3,500 U.S. Marines come ashore. Although it is claimed that these troops are there only to protect U.S. installations at Da Nang and two other locales, this now definitely establishes a commitment of U.S. combat troops.
- *March 24:* The first "teach-in" is held at the University of Michigan. This practice—of canceling regular classes and holding marathon sessions devoted to discussions about the war—soon spreads among U.S. college and universities.
- *March 30:* Vietcong bomb the U.S. Embassy in Saigon, killing two Americans.
- *May:* The U.S. Navy's "Operation Market Time" begins along South Vietnam's coast. This is a major commitment of U.S. ships to halt North Vietnamese shipping.
- *May 3:* The 173rd Airborne Brigade becomes the first army combat force deployed in Vietnam.
- *June 11:* A new military junta takes over South Vietnam, led by Air Vice Marshal Nguyen Cao Ky.
- *June 9:* Troops from Australia, the first of 15 Pacific allies to send units, arrive.
- *June 10–13:* The United States's Dong Xoai operations center is attacked.
- *June 18:* The first Guam-based B-52 bombers strike targets in South Vietnam.
- *June 27–30:* The 173rd Airborne begins the first U.S. offensive, with one soldier killed.
- *July 2:* Planes from the USS *Oriskany* hit oil storage tanks south of Hanoi.
- *July 24:* A Soviet-built SAM missile downs a U.S. plane over North Vietnam.
- *July 28:* President Johnson announces a troop increase to 125,000. The "Screaming Eagles" 101st Airborne Division arrives in Vietnam.
- *August:* U.S. troops operating alone for the first time, destroy 700 Vietcong outside their Chu Lai base in what is known as Operation Starlite. The First Air Cavalry defeats North Vietnamese Army (NVA) soldiers who attack the Plei Me Special Forces site.
- *August 5:* The Reverend Martin Luther King, by now the admired leader of the civil rights struggle in the United States, speaks out

against President Johnson's policies in Vietnam. As the war continues, King will increasingly link the social and economic issues at home with the government's involvement in Vietnam.

- *August 13:* ARVN soldiers kill more than 250 Vietcong in the Mekong Delta.
- *October 27–28:* "Silver Bayonet," a major U.S. operation in Ia Drang Valley, starts.
- *November 14:* The Seventh Cavalry's First Battalion lands by helicopter in the Ia Drang Valley and engages NVA troops. The Fifth Cavalry's Second Battalion comes to their aid.
- *November 18:* In the Ia Drang Valley, the most fiercely fought battle so far between U.S. and insurgent forces ends with the North Vietnamese withdrawing, but U.S. soldiers are not allowed to pursue them into Cambodia.
- *December 25:* Johnson temporarily ends bombing in North Vietnam, hoping for negotiations.
- *December 31:* The U.S. military presence in Vietnam has reached 184,300; this year, 1,369 U.S. personnel have died.

1966

- *January 6:* Vietcong attack Khe Sanh, using 120mm mortars for the first time.
- *January 24–March 6:* In a major search-and-destroy operation, the First Air Cavalry, with ARVN, South Korean, and U.S. Marines support, blanket Binh Dinh Province. U.S. dead total 350, and 2,000 are wounded.
- *March 9–11:* An enemy attack destroys Ashau Special Forces camp, killing five Americans.
- *April 1:* A Saigon hotel is bombed by the Vietcong, killing three American soldiers.
- *April 12:* Vietcong attack Tan Son Nhut Air Base with mortar fire, killing seven U.S. soldiers. U.S. B-52s bomb North Vietnam for the first time.
- *June 20:* After renewed, violent Buddhist demonstrations, Premier Ky agrees to elections.
- *July 15–August 3:* Operation Hastings employs 11,000 ARVN and U.S. soldiers in Quang Tri Province. The U.S. forces suffer some 300 dead, 1,500 wounded.

- *September 14:* U.S. forces torch the village of Lienhoa with matches, according to reporters present. Military officials claim air strikes and artillery razed the village.
- *October 16–November 12:* Tay Ninh Province is the site of Operation Attleboro, involving 20,000 ARVN and U.S. combatants and 2,500 sorties by U.S. planes. The U.S. forces report some 400 killed.
- *October 19:* In a speech before the Senate, Senator George Aiken of Vermont puts forth his solution to the war in Vietnam: "Declare the United States the winner and begin de-escalation."
- *December 31:* The number of U.S. military personnel in Vietnam reaches 280,000. Another 60,000 are on board nearby ships and 35,000 are in Thailand. This year's U.S. death toll passes 5,000, with more than 30,000 wounded.

1967

- *January 2:* U.S. F-4 Phantom jets destroy seven enemy MiG-21s near Red River Delta sites of SAMs.
- *January 8–26:* Operation Cedar Falls roots out insurgents around Saigon.
- *January 25:* After growing criticism, U.S. pilots are ordered not to bomb the center of Hanoi.
- *February 22–April 15:* To wipe out a Vietcong enclave near Cambodia, Operation Junction City sends in 27,000 U.S. and ARVN soldiers. General Westmoreland describes this as "one of the most successful single actions of the year," but some 600 U.S. soldiers are killed and 2,000 wounded.
- *February 27:* The United States's Da Nang air force base is shelled by Vietcong.
- *March 10–11:* U.S. bombers hit the Thainguyen foundry north of Hanoi.
- *April 6:* NVA troops and Vietcong attack Quang Tri City near the Demilitarized Zone (DMZ).
- *April 24–May 5:* U.S. Marines hold off NVA forces near Khe Sanh airstrip but lose 160 men.
- *June 2:* NVA forces attack U.S. Marines outside Da Nang.
- *July 15:* The Da Nang air base is hit by rockets; 12 U.S. personnel are killed.
- *July 29:* A flash fire kills 134 on aircraft carrier *Forrestal* in the worst U.S. naval disaster since World War II.

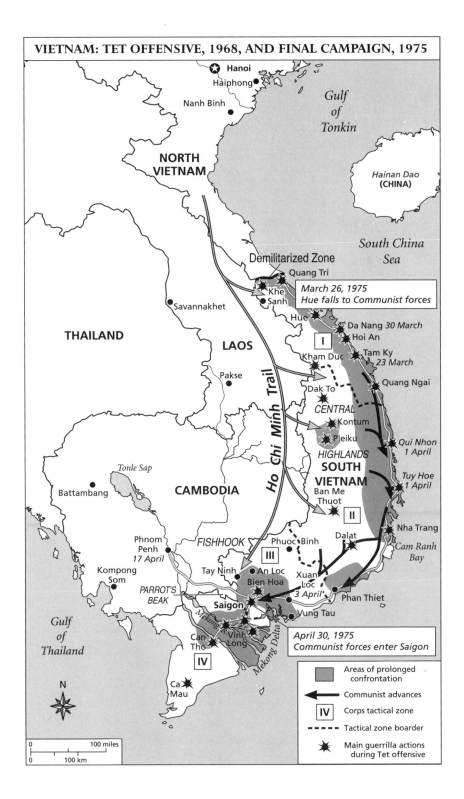

VIETNAM: TET OFFENSIVE, 1968, AND FINAL CAMPAIGN, 1975

Hanoi

Haiphong

Nanh Binh

NORTH VIETNAM

Gulf of Tonkin

Hainan Dao (CHINA)

South China Sea

Demilitarized Zone

Quang Tri

Khe Sanh

March 26, 1975
Hue falls to Communist forces

Savannakhet

Hue

Da Nang *30 March*

Hoi An

THAILAND

LAOS

I

Kham Duc

Tam Ky *23 March*

Dak To

Quang Ngai

Pakse

CENTRAL

Kontum

Pleiku

Qui Nhon *1 April*

HIGHLANDS

SOUTH VIETNAM

Tonle Sap

Tuy Hoe *1 April*

Battambang

CAMBODIA

Ban Me Thuot

II

Nha Trang

Cam Ranh Bay

Phnom Penh *17 April*

FISHHOOK

Phuoc Binh

Dalat

Kompong Som

Tay Ninh

III

An Loc

Bien Hoa

Xuan Loc *3 April*

PARROT'S BEAK

Saigon

Phan Thiet

Gulf of Thailand

Vung Tau

Can Tho

Vinh Long

April 30, 1975
Communist forces enter Saigon

IV

Ca Mau

N

	Areas of prolonged confrontation
←	Communist advances
IV	Corps tactical zone
- - -	Tactical zone boarder
✸	Main guerrilla actions during Tet offensive

0   100 miles

0   100 km

- *September 3:* In South Vietnamese elections, Gen. Nguyen Van Thieu becomes president; Marshal Ky is elected vice president.
- *October:* Polls register a major change in U.S. public opinion, with more opposing the war than favoring it.
- *October 21–23:* More than 50,000 antiwar demonstrators rally at the Pentagon.
- *October 27:* Father Philip Berrigan, a Roman Catholic priest, breaks into a Selective Service office in Baltimore and pours ducks' blood over draft records. He is arrested but released on bond. On May 17, 1968, he and his brother Daniel, a fellow priest, break into another Selective Service office in Catonsville, Maryland, and this time they burn draft records. Philip will serve about three years for his actions, Daniel less than two.
- *October 29–November 3:* U.S. forces at Loc Ninh beat off an attack by NVA troops; the United States claims to have killed 900 of the enemy, but such "body counts" are coming under increasing suspicion.
- *December 31:* U.S. troops reach 500,000, with an additional 100,000 on board ships and in Thailand. U.S. fatalities surpass 9,000, with nearly 100,000 wounded.

1968

- *January 20–April 6:* NVA troops conduct a siege of the Khe Sanh marine installation.
- *January 31–February 25:* NVA and Vietcong soldiers initiate their most serious attack yet at Tet, the lunar new year, and previously a time of truce. The Vietcong hit U.S. airfields and bases from the DMZ to the Mekong Delta, capturing many provincial centers. Coming at a time when U.S. military and government officials have been claiming that the war is well under control, the Tet Offensive causes a drastic loss of both popular and high-level support: The issue now becomes how to end U.S. involvement.
- *February 7:* Equipped with Soviet tanks, the NVA overruns Langvei Special Forces post.
- *February 14:* The Hanoi area receives heavy U.S. bombardment.
- *February 26:* U.S. and South Vietnamese forces recapture Hue, ending the Tet Offensive.
- *February 27:* TV news anchor Walter Cronkite, generally regarded as one of the most trusted men in the United States, voices his doubts

A wounded soldier is treated on the battlefield in Hue during the Tet Offensive, February 1968. *(National Archives)*

about the progress and point of the war. It is believed that this has a major impact on President Johnson's thinking.

- *March 11–April 7:* Twenty-two American and 11 ARVN battalions initiate Operation Quyet Thang in Saigon and five nearby provinces.
- *March 16:* Lt. William Calley leads a platoon of U.S. soldiers in a sweep of My Lai, a hamlet belonging to the village of Songmy. The U.S. forces kill 300 to 500 unarmed villagers. It will be November 17, 1969, before a *New York Times* article reveals this massacre to the public.
- *March 31:* President Johnson announces that he will not run for reelection and that the bombing of North Vietnam will end, except at the DMZ.
- *April 1:* Clark Clifford replaces Robert McNamara as secretary of defense. It is no secret that McNamara has resigned because of his personal discomfort with his own role in the government's policies in Vietnam.
- *April 22:* Secretary Clifford indicates that South Vietnam forces will take a more active role in fighting.
- *May 5–13:* North Vietnamese shell 119 South Vietnamese cities, towns, and military installations.

- *May 25–June 4:* Saigon is the target of a major Vietcong attack.
- *June 10:* Gen. Creighton Abrams takes over command of U.S. troops in Vietnam.
- *August 18:* An attack by the NVA and Vietcong centers on Tay Ninh and Binh Long provinces.
- *August 23:* Rockets and mortars barrage numerous cities and provincial capitals, particularly Hue, Quang Tri, Da Nang's airfield and Duclap.
- *August 26–29:* Violent riots strike Chicago's Democratic National Convention, at which Vice President Hubert Humphrey is nominated for president. It is no secret that Humphrey would like to distance himself from Johnson's policies in Vietnam, but he will be unable to campaign this way.
- *September 13–October 1:* U.S. and ARVN forces initiate a major DMZ foray.
- *November 1:* The U.S. command in Vietnam launches Operation Phoenix, an intelligence-gathering operation using torture and assassinations. All U.S. bombing over North Vietnam stops, but air attacks on the Ho Chi Minh Trail increase.
- *November 5:* Richard Nixon is elected president after indicating that he had some special plan for ending the war in Vietnam. He does promise troop withdrawals, but there is no indication of any alternative to the Johnson policies.
- *November 8–9:* B-52s attack enemy troops in Tay Ninh Province.
- *December 31:* U.S. forces in Vietnam total more than 536,000; there have been nearly 14,600 U.S. fatalities during this year.

1969

- *January 22–March 18:* The U.S. Ninth Marine Regiment goes on the offensive in Operation Dewey Canyon throughout Ashau Valley.
- *January 25:* After nine months of preliminary negotiation, the United States, North Vietnam, and South Vietnam sit down in Paris for the first formal peace talk.
- *February 7:* The U.S. Navy reports 200 enemy deaths along Cape Batangan.
- *February 22:* The Vietnamese New Year cease-fire ends with enemy artillery attacks on Saigon and 70 other cities and military installations.

- *March:* President Richard M. Nixon institutes a policy of "Vietnamization"—that is, requiring the South Vietnamese to take an ever heavier share of the fighting while the United States reduces its military presence.
- *March 18:* Operation Menu, the secret bombardment of Cambodia by the U.S. Air Force, begins. During the next 14 months, U.S. planes will fly some 3,630 sorties and drop 110,000 tons of bombs in Cambodia.
- *March 20:* The "Chicago Eight" —eight political radicals: Rennie Davis, David Dellinger, John Froines, Tom Hayden, Abbie Hoffman, Jerry Rubin, Bobby Seale, and Lee Wiener—are charged with conspiracy to incite riots during the Democratic National Convention in August 1968.
- *April 5–6:* Massive antiwar demonstrations in New York, San Francisco, Los Angeles, and Washington, D.C., demand U.S. withdrawal.
- *May 1–July 16:* Quang Tri Province is the site of Operation Virginia Ridge, conducted by U.S. Marines. U.S. losses include 131 killed and some 700 wounded.
- *May 8:* At the Paris Peace Talks, North Vietnam demands U.S. withdrawal from Vietnam and a coalition government.
- *May 9:* National Security Council adviser Henry Kissinger asks FBI director Herbert Hoover to wiretap reporters and national security affairs staff after the *New York Times* reports the U.S. secret bombing campaign in Cambodia.
- *May 10–20:* Apbia, mountain, called "Hamburger Hill" by U.S. troops, is captured after a bloody battle as part of Operation Apache Snow. The U.S. troops will abandon the hill on May 28.
- *May 11–12:* Enemy artillery hits Saigon, Hue, and 127 other targets.
- *June 5:* U.S. aircraft attack North Vietnam in reprisal for the downing of a U.S. reconnaissance plane.
- *June 8:* President Nixon announces withdrawal of 25,000 U.S. soldiers. The U.S. forces in Vietnam are now at their peak, some 543,000.
- *June 25:* The U.S. Navy gives 64 gunboats to South Vietnam as part of the Vietnamization process.
- *July 11:* The 1968 conviction of Dr. Benjamin Spock, the greatly admired authority on baby care, for conspiracy to counsel resistance to the draft, is overturned by a federal appeals court.
- *July 15–September 25:* The U.S. Third Marine Regiment launches Operation Idaho Canyon in Quang Tri Province.

A member of the First Brigade, Fifth Infantry Division, takes down barbed wire surrounding the command post of Operation Utah Mesa in the A Shau Valley, July 1969. *(National Archives)*

- *August 12:* More than 150 South Vietnamese sites are targeted by NVA and Vietcong forces.
- *August 17–26:* More than 60 U.S. soldiers die in fighting south of Da Nang.
- *September 3:* North Vietnam's leader, Ho Chi Minh, dies at age 79.
- *September 16:* President Nixon announces withdrawal of 35,000 more troops.
- *September 19:* President Nixon lowers the year's draft quota by 50,000.
- *October 10:* The South Vietnamese navy acquires 80 U.S. Navy river-patrol boats.
- *November 12:* Lt. William Calley is charged with crimes against civilians resulting from the My Lai Massacre (March 16, 1968).
- *November 13–15:* Antiwar demonstrators in San Francisco and Washington, D.C., demand a moratorium on the Vietnam War. The climax comes on November 15, when 250,000 march in Washington, the largest antiwar demonstration in U.S. history.

- *December 15:* The U.S. government announces it will withdraw 50,000 more troops. As increasing numbers of U.S. military personnel are now visible in transit in the United States, some of them complain that they are being harassed, even spit on, by young people opposed to the war.
- *December 31:* U.S. fatalities in 1969 dropped to fewer than 9,500. "Fragging" attacks on officers, (so named because enlisted men often tossed Fragmentation grenades at unpopular officers) increased over the year, and there were 117 convictions for mutiny and refusal to follow orders. Drug use among the U.S. troops is rampant.

1970

- *January 26:* NVA forces shell 29 South Vietnamese locations.
- *January 28:* In response to attack of a reconnaissance plane, the U.S. bombs a North Vietnamese missile base.
- *January 31–February 1:* Enemy fire continues on 100 sites throughout the Mekong Delta to the DMZ.
- *February 2:* U.S. bombers target North Vietnamese antiaircraft sites.
- *February 14:* A Gallup poll indicates that 55 percent of those Americans polled still oppose an immediate withdrawal of U.S. troops from Vietnam.
- *February 17–19:* U.S. planes hit North Vietnamese troops in Laos, causing congressional criticism.
- *February 19:* The Chicago Seven are acquitted (Black Panther Bobby Seale has separated his trial from the others).
- *February 20:* National Security Council Advisor Henry Kissinger and North Vietnam's Le Duc Tho begin secret talks in Paris.
- *March 20:* Cambodia calls in U.S. planes and ARVN artillery to rebuff the enemy.
- *April 1:* Vietcong forces attack 115 South Vietnamese targets.
- *May 1–2:* North Vietnamese depots and other sites are bombed by hundreds of U.S. planes.
- *May 9:* More antiwar protests occur at U.S. colleges, and up to 100,000 protesters march in Washington, D.C.
- *April 30:* President Nixon agrees to send nearly 8,000 U.S. soldiers into Cambodia.
- *May 2–4:* In response to the new incursion into Cambodia, antiwar protests occur at colleges. At Kent State University in Ohio, four student demonstrators are shot and killed by National Guardsmen.

- *May 9:* U.S. and South Vietnamese gunboats pursue the enemy on the Mekong River.
- *May 19:* North Vietnamese artillery fire on 60 South Vietnamese sites.
- *September 5–October 8:* U.S. troops conduct their last major assault, Operation Jefferson Glen, in Thau Thien Province. By the end, the United States reports 200 killed, 700 wounded
- *October 7:* President Nixon proposes a cease-fire throughout all of Indochina and then a peace conference to settle all issues. He states that the United States will withdraw all its forces but that any agreements must be approved by the South Vietnamese.
- *November 21:* Ten U.S. helicopters make a covert landing outside Hanoi to liberate U.S. prisoners but find none. More than 200 U.S. aircraft bomb North Vietnamese targets, the heaviest air assault in almost two years.
- *December 1:* South Vietnamese troops launch an attack in the southern Mekong Delta.
- *December 2:* Enemy rockets hit 22 South Vietnamese locations.
- *December 30:* The U.S. Navy turns over 125 boats to South Vietnam's navy, ending U.S. participation on South Vietnam's inland waterways.
- *December 31:* President Nixon signs the repeal of the Tonkin Gulf Resolution; up to now, Congress has allowed the presidents to conduct the war under its aegis. As the year comes to an end, almost 335,000 U.S. soldiers remain in Vietnam. The year's U.S. fatalities, 4,204, is the lowest number since 1965.

1971

- *January 3:* U.S. bombers attack enemy positions in Laos, Cambodia, and South Vietnam.
- *January 6:* The U.S. military institutes an antidrug program.
- *February 8–March 24:* ARVN forces conduct Operation Lam Son 719. It will become known as the bloodiest fighting of the war. It ends with both sides claiming victory.
- *March 1:* A radical group calling itself the Weather Underground explodes a bomb at the U.S. Capitol.
- *March 20:* Indicative of the increasing resistance by U.S. troops to risk their lives in what they regarded as a futile war, 53 U.S. soldiers

refuse to recover a helicopter and armored vehicle from near Laos. The men are reassigned, but no further disciplinary action is taken.

- *March 29:* Lieutenant Calley is convicted of premeditated murder for his role in the My Lai massacre, although his life sentence is reduced to 20 years.
- *April 18–23:* U.S. planes carry out a heavy air raid on North Vietnam.
- *April 24:* Hundreds of thousands of antiwar demonstrators, including Vietnam veterans, crowd Washington, D.C., and San Francisco.
- *May 3–5:* More than 12,000 protesters are arrested in Washington, D.C., the largest number ever jailed for civil disobedience in the nation.
- *May 16–18:* Enemy artillery hits DMZ sites.
- *June 13:* The *New York Times* publishes the so-called Pentagon Papers, surreptitiously photocopied by Daniel Ellsberg, a massive collection of secret documents that reveal how the government has been telling less than the full truth about U.S. involvement in Vietnam.
- *June 30:* The Supreme Court rules that newspapers can print classified Pentagon documents. Use of all herbicides, including Agent Orange, stops in South Vietnam.
- *July 9:* ARVN forces take full responsibility below the DMZ.
- *July 17:* Nixon's chief of staff, John Ehrlichman, puts together a secret group to collect information on Daniel Ellsberg and others regarded by the administration as undermining the nation's policies.
- *October 3:* South Vietnamese leader Thieu is reelected president.
- *November 12:* President Nixon states U.S. ground troops will remain in Vietnam only as a defensive force.
- *December 26:* U.S. aircraft resume raids on North Vietnam, in the largest increase for more than three years.
- *December 31:* With the U.S. presence now at 156,800, American fatalities number fewer than 2,000 this year.

1972

- *January 1:* U.S. aircraft hit Cambodian and Laotian targets.
- *February 9:* The USS *Constellation* joins other U.S. aircraft carriers off Vietnam.
- *March 23:* The United States suspends peace talks.
- *March 30:* The NVA starts the Eastertide Offensive, capturing northern Quang Tri Province.

- *April 3–10:* Three U.S. aircraft carriers—the *Kitty Hawk, Saratoga,* and *Midway*—arrive off Vietnam to convey the message that the United States remains committed to supporting South Vietnam.
- *April 13:* Enemy attacks, the heaviest since the 1968 Tet Offensive, are launched on 107 different targets in South Vietnam.
- *April 15:* Hanoi and Haiphong are once again subject to regular U.S. bombing.
- *April 25:* Enemy forces gain control along the Cambodian-Vietnam border east of the Mekong River.
- *May–October:* Operation Linebacker I provides U.S. air support to ARVN troops.
- *May 2:* Continuing secret meetings, Kissinger tells Tho that the United States will not require North Vietnamese withdrawal from South Vietnam.
- *May 8:* President Nixon announces increased bombing of North Vietnam and mining of Haiphong and other North Vietnamese ports.
- *June 17:* Five men are arrested burglarizing the Democratic National Committee's office in the Watergate Hotel; as the full story unfolds and expands, it will become known as "Watergate."
- *June 18:* Enemy troops withdraw from An Loc.
- *August 23:* The last U.S. combat ground force, the Third Battalion, Twenty-first Infantry, leaves.
- *October 8:* Kissinger and Tho agree on a tentative peace plan.
- *October 22:* Kissinger is in Saigon, trying to get President Thieu to agree to the terms worked out in Paris. Thieu refuses.
- *October 24:* The Paris Peace Talks lead to cessation of U.S. air raids on North Vietnam.
- *October 26:* At a White House news conference, Kissinger states that "We believe peace is at hand." He will later be accused of misrepresenting the situation in order to advance Nixon's bid for reelection.
- *November 7:* President Nixon soundly defeats George McGovern.
- *November 11:* Ending U.S. Army combat operations, the U.S. base at Long Binh is taken over by the ARVN.
- *December 18–31:* With Operation Linebacker II, the United States undertakes its heaviest bombing of Hanoi yet. The North Vietnamese respond with some 1,200 missiles, taking down 15 B-52s and leaving 93 flyers dead, wounded, or missing.
- *December 31:* U.S. forces in Vietnam drop to little more than 24,000, but fatalities for the year reach 4,300.

1973

- *January 15:* Expecting an armistice, President Nixon stops all U.S. offensives against North Vietnam, including the bombing raids.
- *January 18–26:* Combat continues in South Vietnam as both sides vie to gain the advantage before a truce is declared.
- *January 27:* A peace accord is signed in Paris, and the U.S. military draft ends. Lt. Col. William B. Nolde is killed 11 hours before the cease-fire goes into effect, the last U.S. combat fatality in Vietnam.
- *March 29:* The U.S. military closes its Vietnam headquarters. All U.S. combat forces leave, and Hanoi releases 590 prisoners of war. The U.S. government at this time claims there are only about 1,270 personnel missing in action (known as MIAs), but some people claim there are far more. As the years pass, the government will revise that figure upward to about 1,600, even as hundreds of bodies are discovered and returned, but the issue of the Vietnam War MIAs continues to disturb some Americans.
- *July:* The U.S. finishes mine removal in North Vietnamese harbors as part of the cease-fire agreement.
- *August 15:* U.S. bombing raids in Cambodia have continued but finally end on this day, thus ending all American military action in Indochina.
- *November 7:* Congress overrides President Nixon's veto of the War Powers Act, ending his ability to send soldiers abroad without congressional approval.
- *December 31:* Fifty American military personnel remain in Vietnam.

1974

- *March:* The most fighting takes place since the January 1973 cease-fire.
- *July 30:* Acting upon the revelations of the Watergate scandal, the House Judiciary Committee votes to impeach President Nixon.
- *August 9:* President Nixon resigns. Vice President Gerald Ford assumes the presidency.
- *September 16:* Ford issues a presidential proclamation, offering clemency to Vietnam draft evaders and deserters.
- *September 20:* Violent protests against the government take place in Saigon.

- *December 3:* The NVA attacks ARVN targets in Phuoc Long Province.
- *December 31:* Fifty Americans remain in Vietnam, and South Vietnam reports the highest fatalities yet, 80,000.

1975

- *January 6:* NVA forces take over Phuoc Long Province.
- *January 8:* The NVA launches a major attack on South Vietnam.
- *March 10–31:* With wholescale ARVN desertions, the town of Banmethuot is overrun by the NVA. In the next two weeks, the NVA forces proceed to rush southward as the NVA forces retreat. By April 1, the NVA is in control of northern South Vietnam and it will continue the advance on Saigon.
- *April 23:* President Ford announces the war is finished "as far as America is concerned."

Dedicated in 1982, the Vietnam Veterans Memorial in Washington, D.C., bears the names of more than 50,000 U.S. fatalities. *(Library of Congress, Prints & Photographs Division [HABS-805-12-307601])*

- *April 25:* President Thieu escapes to Thailand.
- *April 29:* NVA troops storm Saigon. Marine corporal Charles McMahon, Jr., and Lance Corporal Darwin Judge, the last two Americans killed, die from shrapnel from a NVA rocket.
- *April 29–30:* All Americans in Saigon leave in Option IV, the largest helicopter evacuation ever undertaken.

Results

The casualties of the Vietnam War are remarkable, considering how little territory was being fought over. Some 47,244 U.S. personnel were killed in action, another 10,446 died from related causes such as disease and accidents, and more than 300,000 were wounded, many of these maimed for life. The South Vietnamese military losses were about 200,000; the Vietcong and North Vietnamese military lost between 500,000 and 1,000,000; the total number of Vietnamese civilians killed is estimated as at least 1,000,000. No monetary price has ever been assigned to the material damage to Vietnam; the land and infrastructure were devastated and it would take many decades for it to recover. It has been estimated that the war cost the United States some $150 billion, not even counting indirect costs such as those for veterans. Among the latter were the many who suffered from posttraumatic stress disorder (PTSD) and were unable to get their lives back in order.

In other areas, the results were no less profound. On July 26, 1976, the North Vietnamese finally and formally declared a completely united and independent Vietnam, a goal that had never truly been achieved before. The United States, meanwhile, had come to recognize the "Vietnam Syndrome": namely, a wariness, even a fear, of becoming involved in foreign wars, however idealistic the motives. When this syndrome is relevant to making such a decision continues to be debated.

11

THE PERSIAN
GULF WAR

Kuwait, located on the north end of the Persian Gulf and bordered by Iraq and Saudi Arabia, is a small country that owes its modern existence to the British, who in about 1775 chose to make its port city an outpost of their far-flung colonial empire. By the time Kuwait gained its independence from Britain in 1961, it had become rich from the vast quantities of petroleum beneath its largely desert land. Iraq, meanwhile, had long regarded Kuwait as one of its own provinces (as it had been under the Ottoman Empire) and resented being deprived of both Kuwait's petroleum riches and its access to the sea. Not until Saddam Hussein took over as president of Iraq in 1979, however, did Iraq begin to mount increasingly aggressive actions against those it perceived as enemies.

1988

- *March:* Saddam Hussein uses chemical weapons, including nerve gas, on Kurds in northern Iraq. Hussein justifies the attack with the claim that the Kurds have been unfaithful to Iraq during the war with Iran.
- *August 20:* Iran and Iraq agree to a truce that ends their eight years of war. U.S. administrations, both Democratic and Republican, detesting the rulers of Iran, have been providing weapons and aid of various kinds to Iraq during their war.
- *August 25:* Hussein's Iraqi forces begin a major internal campaign against the Kurdish minority.

1989

- Iraq spends some $15 billion on weapons. Even for an oil-rich nation, this represents a staggering amount of the nation's wealth. Meanwhile, Iraq ran up a large debt during its war with Iran, and much of that debt is to Kuwait. Saddam demands that Kuwait forgive that debt because Iraq had been fighting to defend all Arab nations.

1990

- *April 2:* Saddam Hussein vows to "burn half of Israel" if that nation attempts a preemptive strike against his arsenal of chemical weapons. Israel had successfully bombed an Iraqi nuclear installation in 1981.
- *June 4: U.S. News and World Report* profiles Saddam Hussein on its cover. The article is entitled "The World's Most Dangerous Man." *U.S. News* points out that Hussein has an army of about 1 million, making it the fourth largest in the world.
- *July 15–30:* U.S. satellites show that large sections of the Iraqi army have mobilized just north of the border with Kuwait. Most U.S. analysts conclude that Hussein is trying to bluff Kuwait into making concessions.
- *July 25:* The U.S. ambassador to Iraq, April Glaspie, has her first meeting with Saddam Hussein. Glaspie tells Hussein that her government has no position on Arab-to-Arab conflicts. The Iraqi dictator makes plain that he believes the United States does not want to get involved in a fight in the Middle East. Hussein formed this opinion on the basis of the U.S. withdrawal from Lebanon after the deaths of 241 U.S. Marines in a bombing of their barracks in October 1983.
- *August 2:* Iraqi troops suddenly invade Kuwait, moving into Kuwait City by early morning. Tanks, planes, and personnel carriers move swiftly, showcasing the size and might of the Iraqi forces. When word reaches New York, the UN Security Council quickly passes Resolution 660, which condemns the Iraqi invasion and demands an immediate withdrawal from Kuwait.
- *August 3:* President George H. W. Bush tells reporters, "This will not stand," in reference to Hussein's invasion of Kuwait. In Kuwait, Iraqi troops, having dispersed virtually all resistance, are within five miles of the border between Kuwait and Saudi Arabia. In Kuwait City, the Iraqi forces have been killing, raping, and pillaging; Kuwaitis are fleeing the country.

- *August 6:* The UN Security Council passes Resolution 661, asking member nations to support an embargo against Iraq. The U.S. Defense Department orders the deployment of military aircraft and ships to the region.
- *August 9:* Gen. H. Norman Schwarzkopf is named commander of Operation Desert Shield, intended to prevent an Iraqi takeover of Saudi Arabia. Out of courtesy to the Saudis, Prince Khalid Bin Sultan, a general in their army, will be named as joint commander.
- *August 25:* UN Resolution 665 allows member states to halt and inspect ships carrying cargo to Iraq.
- *August 26:* General Schwarzkopf arrives in Saudi Arabia. Known as "the Bear" or "Stormin' Norman," he has an illustrious record in the U.S. Army and sound knowledge of the Middle East.
- *August:* President Bush conducts telephone diplomacy from Washington, D.C., and his vacation home in Maine. Capitalizing on contacts from his days in the Central Intelligence Agency and Foreign Service, Bush swiftly enlists international support against Iraq. Known as the Coalition, it will eventually enlist 34 nations to provide some form of military support and 14 others to provide financial or other aid. The main combatants, in addition to the United States, are Britain, Saudi Arabia, France, Egypt, and Syria.
- *September–October:* Nearly 210,000 U.S. soldiers are settled into their bases in Saudi Arabia.
- *October:* President Bush's advisers warn him that an all-out war to liberate Kuwait would cost about 36,000 American lives. Among those cautioning a slow and solid approach to entering on such a war is Gen. Colin Powell, chairman of the Joint Chiefs of Staff.
- *November 8:* President Bush announces his intention to double the number of U.S. troops committed to Desert Shield.
- *November 21–24:* Bush arrives in the Middle East and hold a series of meetings with prominent Arab leaders.
- *November 29:* With Resolution 678, the UN Security Council votes to authorize the use of force to expel Iraq from Kuwait unless Iraq withdraws all its forces by January 15, 1991. On the same day, Hussein tells an Arab youth group that "Iraq is neither shaken nor panicked by the air and sea fleets of America and its aides."
- *November–January:* Diplomatic initiatives continue on both sides. In particular, the Russians, who have reluctantly supported the United

A platoon leader conducts a roll call before his soldiers board an aircraft bound for the Persian Gulf region for Operation Desert Shield. *(National Archives/DOD-March ARB)*

States in this matter, try desperately to negotiate some kind of compromise, but time will run out on them.

- *December 19:* General Schwarzkopf estimates, in an internal memo, that it will cost about 20,000 casualties, including 7,000 killed, to liberate Kuwait.

1991

- *January 1:* By this date, there are more than 350,000 U.S. troops and about 250,000 troops from other members of the Coalition forces gathered in Saudi Arabia.
- *January 8:* Former president Richard Nixon announces his support of President Bush's policy in a nationwide editorial.
- *January 9:* Secretary of State James Baker meets Iraqi foreign minister Tariq Aziz in Geneva. Aziz refuses to believe that the United States will follow through on its threat to enforce UN Resolution 678.
- *January 12:* The U.S. Congress debates President Bush's request for "all necessary means" to enforce UN Resolution 678. The House of Representatives approves by a vote of 250 to 183; the Senate approves

by a vote of 52-47. The voting reveals a marked difference between older members of Congress (many of whom had served in World War II) and younger ones (many of whom had served in Vietnam)—the former generally voting to support military action, the latter generally voting against it. Public opinion polls at this time show that 63 percent of Americans support military action, although support falls to 44 percent if those polled are told that U.S. dead might total 1,000, and to only 35 percent if told 10,000 U.S. deaths might result.

- *January 16:* Iraqi media reports that Saddam Hussein has drafted a letter to President Bush, and that the letter begins: "enemy of God and colleague of the devil . . . Accursed be you and hopeless are your objectives." In a radio address to Iraqis this day, Saddam refers to the coming "mother of all battles."
- *January 16–17:* The midnight deadline has elapsed, and no Iraqis have left Kuwait. Operation Desert Shield becomes Operation Desert Storm as Coalition forces begin an around-the-clock bombardment of the Iraqi positions in Kuwait and of the Iraqi homeland. In just the first day, Coalition forces fly more than 1,300 sorties. U.S. naval ships also fire more than 100 Tomahawk missiles into Iraq, the first use of this weapon in combat. Although it will be weeks before the Coalition

Flight deck crew aboard the aircraft carrier USS *Saratoga* watch an EA-6B Intruder aircraft take off during Operation Desert Storm. Coalition forces took advantage of their air superiority to limit the enemy threat to soldiers on the ground. *(National Archives/DOD-March ARB)*

command learns the truth, most of Iraq's command and control operations are seriously wounded on the first day. Coalition forces lose eight aircraft on this first day of the air war. One of the more extraordinary aspects of this event is that Cable News Network (CNN) reporters Peter Arnett and Bernard Shaw are able to televise live coverage of the attack during the first 16 hours.

- *January 18:* Iraq fires Scud missiles at Israel. Six hit Tel Aviv and one hits Haifa. Israelis are outraged and demand action, but the Israeli government honors the U.S. request for Israel to refrain from action. If Israel took military action, the Coalition, composed of Western and Muslim nations, might very quickly have broken apart.
- *January 27–February 1:* About 75 Iraqi air force planes flee Iraq and land in neutral Iran. Even though the two countries had fought an eight-year war in the 1980s, Iran now offers safe haven to the Iraqi planes.
- *February 1:* By this date, the Coalition forces have achieved almost total command in the air over Iraq. They have dropped more explosives on Iraq and Kuwait than the Allies used in six years of World War II. The Coalition's bombing raids continue.
- *February 13:* Two U.S. fighter-bombers attack and destroy a bunkerlike structure near Baghdad. More than 400 civilians are killed. The U.S. insists it was used as a control center, but the Iraqis claim it was a bomb shelter. Iraqi propaganda makes much of the incident.
- *February 22:* President Bush issues an ultimatum to Saddam, threatening an attack by ground forces by 8 P.M. on February 23 (local time). By now Iraqi forces have begun blowing up and setting fire to Kuwaiti oil wells.
- *February 24:* At 4 A.M., U.S. and Coalition forces begin a massive encirclement of the Iraqi troops in Kuwait. One contingent move directly across the Saudi border into Kuwait, heading for Kuwait City. Another group moves into Iraq from a northwesterly direction in a daring sweep designed to outflank the Iraqi forces and cut off their retreat. The main force moves into Iraq between these two. By the end of the first day, it is quite clear that the Iraqi army is totally unable to cope with the Coalition's superiority in weapons, training, and morale; Iraqi troops are surrendering by the thousands.
- *February 25:* As the Coalition forces continue to advance, Saddam recalls his elite Republican Guard forces from Kuwait. They are stationed to the rear of his army and move back into Iraq in the direc-

tion of Basra. Thousands more of the regular Iraqi troops are surrendering. The Coalition forces are taking light casualties, but almost 600 Kuwaiti oil wells are now burning. This day, too, a Scud missile hits a U.S. barracks in Dhahran, Saudi Arabia; 28 U.S. personnel are killed and 90 others are injured.

- *February 26:* As the entire Iraqi army begins a headlong retreat northward, the Iraqis are pounded from the air by U.S. planes. The road leading north from Kuwait to Iraq becomes a disaster zone as U.S. air attacks blast Iraqi military vehicles and civilian cars stolen from the Kuwaiti. It will later be learned that not many more than 200 Iraqi personnel are killed by these attacks, but that is only because they flee in retreat. In tank battles between U.S. forces and those of the elite Republican Guard, the U.S. destroy numerous Iraqi tanks. As Coalition forces close in on Kuwait City, Kuwaiti resistance fighters claim they are now in control of the city.

- *February 27:* The last furious battles are fought inside Iraq. Republican Guard armored divisions clash with U.S. armor. Despite fierce

A Coalition vehicle drives along a road in the Kuwaiti desert with burning oil fields in the background. As Iraqi forces retreated they set fire to oil wells, and the fires burned for months after the war ended. *(National Archives/DOD-March ARB)*

resistance by the Iraqi's elite armored divisions of the Republican Guard, U.S. forces dominate every confrontation between tanks. In one such, the Battle of Medina Ridge, the Americans destroy 61 Iraqi tanks and some 240 other vehicles at the cost of only three American tanks. President George Bush announces that Kuwait has been liberated and calls an end to the Coalition operations at 8 A.M. (local time), February 28, just 100 hours after the offensive began.

- *February 28:* U.S. forces launch one final attack against an Iraqi armored division before halting at 8 A.M. Iraq informs the UN that it agrees to accept the terms of all their resolutions.

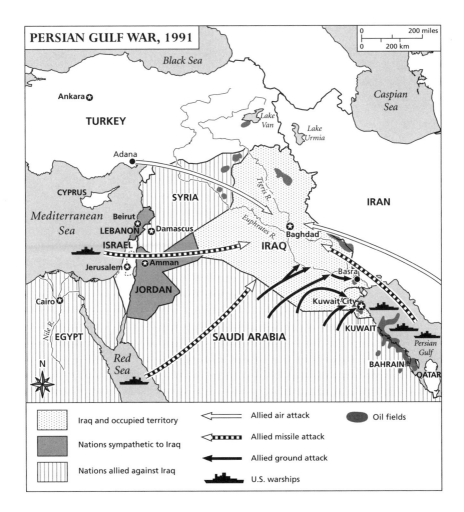

PERSIAN GULF WAR, 1991

Iraq and occupied territory	Allied air attack
Nations sympathetic to Iraq	Allied missile attack
Nations allied against Iraq	Allied ground attack
Oil fields	U.S. warships

Gen. H. Norman Schwarzkopf, commander in chief of U.S. forces, and Lt. Gen. Khalid Bin Sultan Bin Abdul Aziz, commander of the joint forces in Saudi Arabia, discuss cease-fire conditions with Iraqi generals in the final hours of Operation Desert Storm. *(National Archives/DOD-March ARB)*

- *March 2:* Iraqi armored units try to escape from Basra in a violation of the cease-fire agreement. U.S. forces pounce on them and destroy some 600 vehicles and artillery pieces.
- *March 3:* Coalition and Iraqi military leaders meet at an airfield in southern Iraq. The Iraqis, led by Lt. Gen. Hashim Ahmad Al-Jabburi, agree to all the U.S. demands, including a one-kilometer separation between the two sides.
- *Mid-March:* About 100,000 Kurds, serving in the Iraqi militia, revolt against Hussein's regime. The Kurds hope for assistance from the Coalition, but President Bush insists that the UN mandate was only to eject the Iraqis from Kuwait not to topple Saddam Hussein or create a new Kurdish state.
- *March 30:* By this date, Iraqi forces have suppressed the Kurdish rebellion.
- *April 4:* U.N. Security Council Resolution 687 requires that Iraq's weapons of mass destruction be destroyed, and that an international team of inspectors certify the act.

Results

Coalition forces suffered 240 dead and 788 wounded in action; of these, U.S. losses were 148 dead (35 by "friendly fire," or accidental attacks by their own or Coalition forces) and 470 wounded. Four of the dead were women; this was the first time that female U.S. personnel had directly participated in combat operations. Iraqi casualties are uncertain, but it seems likely that at least 100,000 people, both civilians and military, were killed either in the aerial bombardments or in the three days of fighting. The direct cost of the war to the Coalition was some $61 billion, of which the United States paid some $7.5 billion. The cost to Kuwait, including the losses of its oil production, was at least $240 billion, to Saudi Arabia, some $70 billion; and to Iraq, at least $120 billion. The economic sanctions against Iraq remained in place after the war was over, and millions of Iraqis continued to suffer malnutrition or inadequate health care since 1991.

The war clearly established the U.S. superiority in the use of new high-tech weapons and seemed to demonstrate that an intense air campaign could make ground operations much easier. Although it won a tremendous and swift victory, the United States had not removed Saddam Hussein from power. In the years that followed, he continued to threaten world peace simply by virtue of remaining in power; he also was able eventually to drive out the UN-sanctioned weapons inspection team. By its decisive action, however, the UN had at least demonstrated that it would not sit by as one powerful nation attacked its weaker neighbor.

Glossary

abolitionism   In the decades leading up to the Civil War, a movement that called for an immediate end to slavery, as opposed to the desire of most northerners, including Lincoln, for the restriction of the institution of slavery to states where it already existed.

ace   The term for a flyer who shoots down five planes or more in aerial combat.

amphibious warfare   The landing of troops and equipment from the sea in boats or vehicles that can move into shallow water; the vehicles are able to travel up onto the beach.

annex   To incorporate by force or administrative decision territory or political unit into another political unit.

armistice   A truce or agreement by warring parties to cease hostilities, at least temporarily but usually with the intention of negotiating a permanent peace.

artillery   A division of the U.S. Army that uses large, crew-operated weapons such as cannons and missiles; the term can be used both of the weapons and of the army unit using them.

blitzkrieg   A German word ("lightning war"), which has become accepted in English, for a swift and sudden movement of armed forces.

blockade   Isolating a port, city, or nation by surrounding it with ships or troops to prevent the passage of traffic or supplies.

border states   During the Civil War, this referred to the slave states along the country's midsection and so bordering the North and the South. Virginia and Tennessee joined the Confederacy. Federal troops kept Delaware, Maryland, Kentucky, and Missouri within the Union, although men from these states fought on the Confederate as well as the Union side.

burgess   In colonial Virginia and Maryland, a member of the lower house of the legislature. The term is derived from the British word for a member of Parliament who represents a borough, or town.

cannonade   A long and heavy firing of artillery.

casualties   In the case of battles, total casualties usually include those killed, wounded, taken prisoner, and missing in action. When reported for an entire war, casualties may also include those who die in non-combat activities and from diseases contracted while in theaters of war.

cavalry   During the 19th century, the division of an army and its personnel who moved about on horseback and usually fought on horseback; in the 20th century the cavalry switched to using motorized vehicles, eventually including helicopters.

coalition   A combination or alliance arranged on a temporary basis, as among wartime allies.

convoy   A group of ships or land vehicles traveling together for mutual protection, sometimes under armed escort.

dismast   To break or knock away the mast of a sailing ship.

division   A large formation of infantry or cavalry. A division is formed when two or more brigades are linked together under a single command. During the history of the U.S. Army, a division's size has varied greatly but has usually been anywhere from 10,000 to 20,000 troops.

dogfight   In aerial warfare, close and intense combat between fighter planes.

embargo   An order from a government prohibiting the movement of merchant ships from or into its own ports. It may also be issued by a government to prohibit trade, whether specific or all kinds, with foreign nations.

fragging   The maiming or killing of one's own superiors—usually officers—by enlisted men, so called because in Vietnam it often involved tossing a fragmentation grenade.

friendly fire   Accidental attacks from weapons (land, sea, air) on one's own or allied military personnel or installations.

garrison   A military post, usually relatively small and remote, and/or the troops stationed at such a post.

guerrilla warfare   A strategy of warfare in which small bands of nonuniformed soldiers harass a larger and better-armed enemy through surprise raids or attacks on supply and communication lines and usually depend on the sympathy of local civilians for information and shelter.

habeas corpus   From the Latin, meaning "you have the body," it refers to a court order requiring that a person being held by the authorities be brought before the court. This is regarded as a fundamental right under American law. Citing his emergency powers, Lincoln controversially suspended the writ of habeas corpus during the Civil War.

immolation   Setting fire to oneself, usually resulting in death.

impressment   During late 1700s and through the War of 1812, this referred to the kidnapping of men, often at sea but also on shore, to serve in the navy. During the Civil War, it referred to the practice of taking supplies or livestock for an army's use, usually with some form of a written promise to pay.

invalided   Incapacitated by injury or illness.

maneuver   In the military, a strategic or tactical movement.

man-of-war   A warship, usually a large one such as a battleship.

militia   Volunteer soldiers who are not part of a regular army but serve during emergencies.

nationalism   Devotion to the interests of one's own nation, including the desire for national independence.

neutrality   The status of a nation that does not participate in a war between other nations.

panhandle   A narrow strip of land projecting from a defined area. Both Texas and Florida have panhandles.

panzer   A German word that has passed into English, meaning an armored vehicle, especially a tank.

parallel   The imaginary line representing degrees of latitude. After World War II, Korea was divided at the 38th parallel, and Vietnam was divided at the 17th.

pontoon   A floating element, often a flat-bottomed boat, used to support a bridge.

preemptive strike   An offensive action taken by armed forces to deter an anticipated attack by an enemy.

quarter To house and feed someone; in the Revolutionary period, this referred specifically to Britain's insistence on the colonists providing quarters to their troops.

reconnaissance A search made for useful military information in the field by means of observation of enemy positions and movements, and the physical landscape upon which battles are likely to occur.

regiment The basic unit of military organization, an infantry regiment in the U.S. Army has varied in composition and size over the decades. It usually has contained at least two battalions and has numbered from about 1,000 to 2,000 personnel.

reparations Enforced compensation in the form of cash, labor, or materials on the part of a defeated nation to other nations or people it is accused of having unjustly harmed in wartime.

reservation In U.S. history, land set aside by the federal government for the exclusive use of Native Americans.

resolution A statement adopted by a legislative body or assembly formally stating an opinion or position.

salient In warfare, a projecting line of battle that moves close to the enemy.

scalp Cutting the skin from the top of the head of a defeated enemy. It was practiced by both Native Americans and non-Indians in the course of three centuries of wars in North America. When that skin was removed, with or without the hair, it served as a trophy or as proof of the death of the human or animal scalped; in fact, some people did survive being scalped if no damage was done to the brain.

search-and-destroy In the Vietnam War, the name for the strategy adopted by the U.S. ground forces of constantly dispatching units to seek out and attack the enemy rather than waiting for major engagements.

sector A section or division of a defensive position.

siege An army's painstaking sealing off of a town or a fortress from all outside contacts and supplies for the purpose of bringing its defenders residents to surrender without requiring the force of arms. The verb form is "to besiege." When the siege has ended, it is said to have been raised.

skirmish A small battle, usually involving small forces but sometimes referring to an engagement in which large forces are avoiding more direct conflict.

squadron A small group of ships that are part of a larger fleet.

SS From the German words *Schutz* and *Staffel*—"defense" and "echelon"—this was the ruthless unit of the Nazi Party and served as the top security force both in Germany and occupied countries.

stalemate A situation in which action by either side is blocked.

strategy The science of planning and directing large-scale military movements designed to bring about the defeat of an enemy.

tactics The arrangement, deployment, and maneuvering of troops in battle, usually in pursuit of a short-range objective such as capturing a position.

territory An administrative unit of land, such as the Northwest Territory, usually headed by a governor. Most territories later achieved statehood; in 2002, Guam, the Virgin Islands, and American Samoa are administered as U.S. territories.

treaty A formal agreement between governments or interested parties. Treaties between the U.S. government and the Plains Indians consistently diminished first the Indians' original homelands and later their reservations.

trench A long, narrow, deep excavation in the ground serving as a shelter for soldiers to protect them from enemy fire.

Further Reading

This selection of books is designed to round out the other volumes in the America at War set and so deliberately aims to supplement, not duplicate, the kinds of books listed in each of those books. The first group here includes a selection of historical dictionaries and encyclopedias that provide handy access to the basic data of the wars—facilitating not a chronological approach, in other words, but an approach by names and topics. The second group is composed of historical atlases, for it is generally recognized that one of the best ways to understand wars is to have a graphic version of events. The third group is a selection of books that raise broader issues about these wars; their inclusion here does not signify endorsement of their often provocative positions, but they are chosen to stimulate readers with examples of the many controversial aspects of individual wars.

HISTORICAL DICTIONARIES AND ENCYCLOPEDIAS

Boatner, Mark. *The Civil War Dictionary.* New York: Vintage Books, 1991.
Dunnigan, James F., and Alfred Nofi. *The Pacific War Encyclopedia.* 2 vols. New York: Facts On File, 1998.
Dyal, Donald, ed. *Historical Dictionary of the Spanish-American War.* Westport, Conn.: Greenwood Press, 1996.
Heidler, David Stephen, and Jeanne T. Heidler. *Encyclopedia of the War of 1812.* Santa Barbara, Calif.: ABC-Clio, 2000.
Jones, Terry. *Historical Dictionary of the Civil War.* Lanham, Md.: Scarecrow Press, 2002.
Keenan, Jerry, ed. *Encyclopedia of the Spanish-American and Philippine-American War.* Santa Barbara, Calif.: ABC-Clio, 2002.
Kohn, George C. *Dictionary of Wars.* Revised edition. New York: Facts On File, 1999.
Mays, Terry. *Historical Dictionary of the American Revolution.* Lanham, Md.: Scarecrow Press, 1999.

Moise, Edwin E. *Historical Dictionary of the Vietnam War.* Lanham, Md.: Rowman & Littlefield, 2001.
Moseley, Edward H., and Paul C. Clark, Jr. *Historical Dictionary of the Mexican War.* Lanham, Md.: Scarecrow Press, 1997.
Purcell, L. Edward, and Sarah J. Purcell. *Encyclopedia of Battles in North America, 1517 to 1916.* New York: Facts On File, 2000.
Sandler, Stanley. *Encyclopedia of the Korean War.* New York: Garland, 1998.
Schwartz, Richard Alan. *Encyclopedia of the Persian Gulf War.* Jefferson, N.C.: McFarland, 1998.
Thompson, Peter. *Dictionary of American History.* New York: Facts On File, 2000.
Wells, Anne Sharpe. *Historical Dictionary of World War I.* Lanham, Md.: Scarecrow Press, 1999.
———. *Historical Dictionary of World War II.* Lanham, Md.: Scarecrow Press, 1999.

HISTORICAL ATLASES
Barnes, Ian, and Charles Royster. *The Historical Atlas of the American Revolution.* New York: Routledge, 2000.
Esposito, Vincent, ed. *The West Point Atlas of American Wars 1689–1900.* New York: Henry Holt, 1995.
Ferrel, Robert H., and Richard Naktiel. *Atlas of American History.* 3rd edition. New York: Facts On File, 1995.
Gilbert, Martin. *The Routledge Atlas of the First World War.* New York: Routledge, 2002.
McPherson, James M. *The Atlas of the Civil War.* New York: Hungry Minds, 1994.
Stefoff, Rebecca. *The War of 1812.* North American Historical Atlases series. New York: Benchmark Books, 2001.
Summers, Harry G., and Stanley Karnow. *Historical Atlas of the Vietnam War.* Boston: Houghton Mifflin, 1996.
Symonds, Craig, L., and William J. Clipson. *The Naval Institute Atlas of the American Navy.* Annapolis, Md.: U.S. Naval Institute, 2001.
Waldman, Carl. *Atlas of the North American Indian.* Revised edition. New York: Facts On File, 2000.
Young, Peter, ed. *The Cassell Atlas of the Second World War.* London: Cassell Academic, 2000.

HISTORICAL ISSUES
THE REVOLUTIONARY WAR
Bailyn, Bernard. *The Ideological Origins of the American Revolution.* Cambridge, Mass.: Belknap Press, 1992.

Rhodehamel, John, ed. *The American Revolution: Writings from the War for Independence.* New York: Library of America, 2001.

Wood, Gordon. *Radicalism of the American Revolution.* New York: Random House, 1993.

THE WAR OF 1812

Babcock, K. W. *Rise of American Nationality, 1811–1819.* New York: Haskell House, 1969.

Sheppard, George. *Plunder, Profit, and Paroles: A Social History of the War of 1812 in Upper Canada.* Montreal: McGill-Queen's University Press, 1994.

Watts, Steven. *The Republic Reborn: War and the Making of Liberal America, 1790–1820.* Baltimore: Johns Hopkins University Press, 1987.

THE U.S.-MEXICAN WAR

Francaviglia, Richard. *Dueling Eagles: Reinterpreting the Mexican-American War, 1846–1848.* Fort Worth: Texas Christian University Press, 2000.

Frazier, Donald S., ed. *The United States and Mexico at War: Nineteenth-Century Expansionism and Conflict.* New York: Macmillan Library Reference, 1998.

Leckie, Robert. *From Sea to Shining Sea: From the War of 1812 to the Mexican War, The Saga of American Expansion.* New York: HarperCollins, 1993.

THE CIVIL WAR

Cullen, Jim. *The Civil War in Popular Culture: A Reusable Past.* Washington, D.C.: Smithsonian Institution Press, 1995.

Kennedy, Stetson. *After Appomattox: How the South Won the War.* Gainesville: University Press of Florida, 1995.

McPherson, James, and William J. Cooper, Jr., eds. *Writing the Civil War: The Quest to Understand.* Columbia: University of South Carolina Press, 1998.

THE PLAINS INDIAN WARS

Bird, Elizabeth, ed. *Dressing in Feathers: The Construction of the Indian in American Popular Culture.* Boulder, Colo.: Westview Press, 1996.

Ferguson, R. Brian, ed. *Warfare, Culture and Environment.* Orlando, Fla.: Academic Press, 1984.

Weatherford, Jack. *Native Roots: How the Indians Enriched America.* New York: Fawcett, 1992.

THE SPANISH-AMERICAN WAR

Wei, Deborah, and Rachel Kamel. *Resistance in Paradise: Rethinking 100 Years of U.S. Involvement in the Caribbean and the Pacific.* Philadelphia: American Friends Service Committee, 1998.

Hilton, Sylvia, and Steve Ickringill, eds. *European Perceptions of the Spanish-American War.* New York: Peter Lang, 1999.

Hoganson, Kristin L. *Fighting for American Manhood: How Gender Politics Provoked the Spanish-American and Philippine-American Wars.* New Haven: Yale University Press, 1998.

FURTHER READING

WORLD WAR I

Crook, D. P. *Darwinism, War, and History: The Debate over the Biology of War from the "Origin of Species" to the First World War.* Cambridge, England: Cambridge University Press, 1994.

Matsen, William. *The Great War and the American Novel.* New York: Peter Lang, 1993.

Stevenson, David. *The Outbreak of the First World War: 1914 in Perspective.* New York: St. Martin's Press, 1997.

WORLD WAR II

Kryder, Daniel. *Divided Arsenal: Race and the American State during World War II.* Cambridge, England: Cambridge University Press, 2000.

Martel, Gordon, ed. *The Origins of the Second World War: The A. J. P. Taylor Debate After Twenty-five Years.* Boston: Allen & Unwin, 1986.

Warren, Frank A. *Noble Abstractions: American Liberal Intellectuals and World War II.* Columbus: Ohio State University Press, 1999.

THE KOREAN WAR

Matray, James I. *The Reluctant Crusade: American Foreign Policy in Korea, 1941–1950.* Honolulu: University of Hawaii Press, 1985.

Rose, Lisle. *Roots of Tragedy: The United States and the Struggle for Asia, 1945–1953.* Westport, Conn.: Greenwood Press, 1976.

Stueck, William J. *The Road to Confrontation: American Policy toward China and Korea, 1947–1950.* Chapel Hill: University of North Carolina Press, 1981.

THE VIETNAM WAR

Jason, Philip. *Acts and Shadows: The Vietnam War in American Literary Culture.* Lanham, Md.: Rowman & Littlefield, 2000.

Melling, Phil, and Jon Roper, eds. *America, France, and Vietnam: Cultural History and Ideas of Conflict.* Brookfield, Vt.: Gower, 1991.

Simons, G. L. *Vietnam Syndrome: Impact on U.S. Foreign Policy.* New York: St. Martin's Press, 1998.

THE PERSIAN GULF WAR

Bennett, W. Lance, and David Paletz, eds. *Taken by Storm: The Media, Public Opinion, and U.S. Foreign Policy in the Gulf War.* Chicago: University of Chicago Press, 1994.

Elshtain, Jean Bethke, ed. *But Was It Just?: Reflections on the Morality of the Persian Gulf War.* New York: Doubleday, 1992.

Environment and Natural Resources Policy Division, American Law Division, and the Science Policy Research Division of the Congressional Research Service. *The Environmental Aftermath of the Gulf War: A Report.* Washington: Government Printing Office, 1992.

Index

Page numbers in *italics* indicate a photograph. Page numbers followed by *m* indicate maps. Page numbers followed by *g* indicate glossary entries. Page numbers in **boldface** indicate page ranges for individual wars covered.

INDEX

INDEX

CHRONOLOGY OF WARS

INDEX

INDEX

CHRONOLOGY OF WARS

Turkey 116, 128
Turner, Frederick Jackson 102
Tyler, John 40

U

U-boats. *See* submarine warfare
Uncle Tom's Cabin (Stowe) 67
United Nations
    Korean War 165, 176
    Persian Gulf War 205
    World War II 158, 160, 161
United Nations Security Council 199,
    200, 206
United Nations troops 165, 168–170,
    172–174
U. S. maps 50*m*, 54*m*, 76*m*, 88*m*, 100*m*
U.S.-Mexican War **39–51,** 41*m*, 50*m*

V

Valcour Bay, Battle of 11
Valley Forge 15
V-E Day 159–160
Verdun, France 117, *118,* 125
Versailles, Treaty of 128–130, 131, 177
Vicksburg, Battle of 69–70, 72
"Vietnam Syndrome" 197
Vietnam Veterans Memorial *196*
Vietnam War **177–197,** *181,* 185*m, 190*
V-J Day 160

W

Walker, Walton 166, 169, 170
War of 1812 ix, **25–38,** 29*m,* 36*m*
War Powers Act 195
Warsaw, Poland *133*
Warsaw Ghetto 148

Washington, D.C. 32–33, *33,* 77
Washington, George *6,* 11, *12,* 21, *22,* 24
Washington, William *20*
Watergate 194, 195
Watie, Stand 61, 82
Waxhaws, Battle of 18
Westmoreland, William 180, 184
Weyler y Nicolau, Valeriano 103
Wilderness, Battle of the 75
Wilhelm II (kaiser of Germany) 113, 119,
    128
Williamsburg, Battle of 64
Wilmington, North Carolina 80
Wilson, Henry 67
Wilson, Woodrow 115, 117, 119–124,
    127–129
Winchester, James 28
women in military 207
World War I **113–130,** 114*m,* 127*m,*
    129*m*
World War II **131–161,** 137*m,* 141*m,*
    152*m*
Wounded Knee massacre 101

Y

Yalta Conference 157
Yamamoto, Isokuru 135, 144, 148
York, Alvin 127
Yorktown 21, *22, 62*
Ypres, Battles of 116

Z

Zhou Enlai (Chou En-lai) 167
Zimmermann, Arthur 119
Zimmermann telegram 119